THE OBSERVANT JEW

Rabbi Jonathan Gewirtz

THE OBSERVANT JEW

A refreshing new look at the world

DISTRIBUTED BY

FELDHEIM

HIDDEN DOVE PRESS

Many of the articles were originally published in *The Front Page Magazine* (Rockland County, NY)

ISBN 978-1-59826-111-0

Page layout by Eden Chachamtzedek

DISTRIBUTED BY:
Feldheim Publishers
POB 43163 / Jerusalem, Israel
208 Airport Executive Park
Nanuet, NY 10954
www.feldheim.com

10 9 8 7 6 5 4 3 2 1

Printed in Israel

Dedicated in memory of

Blanche Gewirtz

רבקה בריין בת החבר ר' אליעזר ע"ה

who touched the lives of many
and looked at the world in
her own unique way.

She will be remembered for
her *chesed* and the joy she
found in each day.

FROM HER LOVING FAMILY

HER HUSBAND

Rabbi Jonah Gewirtz

HER CHILDREN

Debra & Shim Kurtz & Family

Miriam & Larry Kramer & Family

Danny & Adina Gewirtz & Family

Rabbi Jonathan & Esther Toby Gewirtz & Family

CONTENTS

Introduction . . . . *xi*

Messages from God

Reflections on a Pencil *3*
Give Me a Sign *6*
Two Signs, One Message *9*
A Tree Grows in Brooklyn *12*
That's the Ticket! *15*
Someday You'll Understand *19*
I Hear Dead People *22*
Marketing and Stuff *25*
And Now a Word from Our Sponsor *29*

Look on the Bright Side

If God Is Your Co-Pilot, Switch Seats *35*
Murphy's Law vs Torah Law *38*
Negativity Stinks! (or: My Life As a Pollyanna) *41*
The Problem with Assuming *45*
That's My Job *49*
A Father's Love *52*
When Life Gives You Lemons *55*

Objects in the Mirror

Swallowing the "Bitter" Pill 61

In the Market for Growth 64

Carrying a Tune 68

Shaliach Mitzvah Money 71

That's What Money Is For 74

Life Is a Highway
  (Or At Least a Highly-Congested Urban Intersection) 78

Objects in Mirror Are Closer Than They Appear 82

One Good Turn 85

What Were You Thinking? 87

What Ever Happened to Dinner Music? 90

Pursuit of Happiness

Impulse Buys 95

Smiley Faces 97

The Secret of Happiness 101

It's High Time We Start Stop-Thinking 104

Waive the Crave 107

Not Small Potatoes 110

You Can't Always Get What You Want
  (But If You Try, Sometimes, You Can Want What You Get) 114

Why Are Yawns Contagious? 117

When I Grow Up, I Want to Be in *Chinuch* 120

JACKPOT! 123

Simchah Gedolah L'hiyos B'Mitzvah 126

One Percent Inspiration 130

Holiday Observances

Purim: Variations on a Theme 135

Purim: The Joy of Purim 138

Pesach: What Kind of Jew Are You? 141

Pesach: Being *Machmir* 144

Shavuos: The Ten-Dollar Gym 147

Three Weeks: I Could Care Less 150

Tisha B'Av: A Time to Build 154

Elul: Preparing for the Days of AAUUGGHH!! 157

Rosh Hashanah: Signs 160

Aseres Yemei Teshuvah: You're Stronger Than You Think
  Divrei Chizuk for the *Yamim Nora'im* 163

Yom Kippur: Getting the Message 167

Sukkos: Turning Over an Old Leaf 171

Chanukah: It's All about the Gifts 175

Instruction Manual for Life

Self-Help (Is) for Dummies 181

Hishtadlus without the Effort 185

The Observant Jew Is on Vacation 188

The Quicksand Paradox 190

I Know What Regret Looks Like 194

The Importance of Mitzvah Notes 197

Life Hangs in the Balance 201

My Own Private Everest 204

The Dangers of Going "On Line" 206

The *Bitachon* Machine 209

A Light unto the Nations

Chasidah 215

Not Seeing the Forest for the "ME"s 218

Give 'Til It Feels Good 222

What Did You Call Me?! 225

The Importance of Being Important 229

Towards Less Picturesque Speech 232

Dark Side of the Moon 236

What Makes a *Kiddush Hashem* 239

Now You're Talking 243

Thoughts from All Over

Caught in the Act 249

My Daddy Is a Fix-It Man 252

All I Need To Know
 I Learned From My Kindergartner 255

The Apple of My "i" 258

The *Tefillin* Connection 261

There's a Sucker Born Every Minute 265

What Can I Do? Job Guidance for a Career in Life 269

The World's DUH-mest Headline 273

In the Blink of an Eye 277

Get a Job 281

More Lessons from the Candy Man 285

INTRODUCTION

IN A WORD — RESPONSIBILITY. It's why we do much of what we do in life — and in Judaism, it's more important to us than our rights. It's why this book was written and why you should read it.

A colleague once told me that when you have an ability, you must respond to it. That's response-ability. *Baruch Hashem* I have been blessed with the ability to write things that touch people's hearts and minds. Because of that, I try to use my gifts for the glory of Heaven and write things that inspire people to be their best selves.

I am also blessed with a unique perspective on the world and I share that in my writing. I firmly believe that we constantly get messages from God and that He wants us to pick them up. That, too, is a responsibility. By looking at the world around us, we can gain so much knowledge, wisdom, and pleasure.

The Observant Jew is a column written about ordinary life and extraordinary reactions. It's about thoughtful people and thoughtless ones, and about turning one into the other — in a good way. Week after week (or month after month, depending on which magazine you're reading it in), I am blessed to be able to share my insights with readers around the world.

Life should be enjoyable. That's why Hashem created us, to give us pleasure. The best way to enjoy it, though, is by following the guidance of the Torah and our sages. By collecting the very best of my previous articles, I've tried to offer my readers a look at the world through my eyes, which may very well be a way you never thought of looking at it. I hope you will find it entertaining, inspirational, and worth reading more than once.

I'd like to thank my parents Rabbi Jonah *shlit"a* and Blanche *a"h* Gewirtz for the upbringing I received which was so instrumental in teaching me the power of words and making me a student of human existence. My mother's sense of adventure and my father's deep analysis of events combined within me so that I look forward to new experiences and look at things from all angles.

My vision was further honed by my wife, Esther Toby, and my children Bracha Devorah and Veeta Miriam who constantly open my eyes to new ways of thinking. I love them all dearly and appreciate their support and patience with all my writing endeavors. I would not be who I am without them.

My family, both through blood and marriage, have also been a part of expanding my worldview and I am grateful for the lessons I have learned.

Thank you to Chaim Saperstein, Shoshana Soroka, and the other editors who regularly publish my articles and help me reach people I would otherwise not be able to, and who give me an outlet for my creative observations.

Thank you to Rabbi Dovid Lewin of Kollel Ahavas Yehonason in Ramat Beit Shemesh for his guidance about which items to include and for pushing me towards publication. Thank you to Rabbi Dovid Winiarz of Survival Through Education for his efforts in sharing my material with others and helping me reach this point. The friendship of both of you means a great deal to me. Special Thanks to Eli Meir Hollander of Feldheim Publishers (where my grandfather *a"h* was actually employed half a century ago!) for his guidance and help in making this book a reality.

Finally, I'd like to thank my readers and fans for their constant comments, feedback, and well-wishes — even the ones who stop me on the street or in the supermarket to say, "Hey! I liked what you wrote last week... um... what was it about again?"

Jonathan Gewirtz
Monsey, NY

THIS PAGE INTENTIONALLY LEFT BLANK

(Feel free to use it to jot down inspirations, comments,
grocery lists, or just tear it out and use it as
a bookmark or for wrapping fish.)

Messages
from God

THE PREMISE FOR my articles is that the things I observe (hence the title "The Observant Jew") are not coincidental or arbitrary. Instead, they are specifically intended to teach me something — either about myself, about God, or about mankind.

The Baal Shem Tov said that when we witness something evil in another person, there are two possible reasons. Either we possess that negative trait ourselves and must work on eradicating it, or we are meant to help the other person somehow.

Whichever is the case, everything we see, hear, or "just happen" to come across, is not an accident, but a message for us from God, waiting to be picked up and integrated into our being.

Like a radio, anyone can pick up these messages, as long as you're willing to tune in. So, sit back, read on, and start getting yourself onto the right wavelength to get your own messages from God.

Reflections on a Pencil

A S I WALKED TO shul this past Shabbos morning, I was struck by something unusual. Well, it wasn't the item that was unusual, but where I saw it. On the sidewalk before me, I noticed a pencil. It was yellow, partially sharpened, and lying on the ground at a bit of an angle to the line of the sidewalk.

I wondered, "Why did I see a pencil here?" The simple answer most of us would give is: "Because someone dropped it there." Maybe if we are extra sensitive, we can imagine some poor schoolchild searching his backpack in vain for this little piece of equipment which slipped to its anonymous oblivion on the pavement. But still I wondered.

Sure, it was there because someone dropped it, but WHY did he drop it? No, I don't mean why it was in his hand, or why was his backpack not zipped tightly. I mean cosmically. Obviously it was dropped so I would see it. So what was the message from Heaven? Why did Hashem find it important that I see a pencil lying on the sidewalk that day? My mind started to race.

A pencil has a point for making marks and an eraser for re-moving them. Maybe I was supposed to think about fixing some errors I've made. A bit ahead, I noticed a fellow walking to shul. I knew that in the past, he had driven to shul (*author's note — I was not in Monsey when this happened.*) Perhaps, I thought, he's done *teshuvah*! Like the eraser on the pencil, he had corrected his ways, and I had to acknowledge this great step and treat him accordingly.

Of course, I thought, when you erase pencil marks, you never entirely remove the impression. You can still see that something had been there. I felt bad that even if he had changed, the previous effects of his *chillul Shabbos* might remain with him. My errors, too, leave an impression. Maybe I need to make sure I don't press as hard when I make mistakes so they'll be easier to get rid of.

Later, as I listened to a youthful guest speaker at shul, I thought about the fact that pencils are the implement of choice for young children. Maybe Hashem was indicating that we must always remain students: ready to learn, ready to hear new things, not thinking we know everything.

I thought about how pencils are rigid, and maybe we have to be more flexible. I imagined a strict teacher rapping his or her students on the knuckles with a pencil — perhaps that was too harsh a way to deal with people, and sometimes maybe I'm too critical of others.

I'm ashamed to say that throughout *davening* that day, various thoughts continued to pass through my mind. I thought about the apocryphal story of the American space program. When they sent men into outerspace, NASA had to deal with the issue of weightlessness. There was not enough pressure to make the ink in a ballpoint pen flow. How would astronauts be able to write things down? They had to keep records, take notes, and do crossword puzzles!

So NASA spent millions of dollars developing a pen that was pressurized internally so it could write in the weightlessness of space, or even upside down right here on Earth. The Israelis, as the story goes, just used a pencil.

It made me think that perhaps Hashem was telling me that problems aren't always as challenging as they seem. Sometimes there's a simple answer just waiting to be found. Perhaps that was the message of my little pencil.

Yes, there were many possible reasons that the *Ribono shel Olam* orchestrated things so I'd see a pencil lying in my path on a Shabbos morning. I don't think it's relevant to this article to figure out which I found to be the most compelling message of the pencil. Instead, I have a question for you:

Why do you think Hashem just had *you* read an article about one?

Give Me a Sign

*W*HILE DRIVING DOWN THE highway one day, I saw a billboard that caught my attention. I think it was supposed to be a verse from the New Testament (I still haven't finished with the old one,) but it had big five-foot-high block letters that read: "WHEN YOU DIE YOU WILL MEET GOD."

"Whoa," said my passenger, "that's scary." I guess that was the point of it, to make people think about the fact that one day they will have to give a *din v'cheshbon*, an accounting, for what they've done or not done in their lives. If you know that at the end of the day you have to face the boss, your workday will be a lot different. But of course, to me, there was more to this message.

"It sure is scary," I concurred. "Can you imagine having to wait until you're dead to meet the *Ribono shel Olam*?" Huh? What did I mean by that?

I understand that to other nations of the world religion is kind of like a pass/fail course: everything is true/false, all or nothing, and it only gets graded at the end of the test. But I don't believe Judaism is like that.

I believe that life is a test, but an open-book one, where you get feedback. When I took my tests for *semichah*, I remember the two *roshei yeshivah* sitting there taking turns peppering me with questions. If I didn't know the answer right away it was okay, as long as I knew where to look for the answer. If I was unclear in my response, they questioned me further. I think life is a lot like that.

We have challenges and choices, and we're expected to make mistakes. However, we are directed to constantly analyze ourselves to determine whether or not we are on the right track. When one gets an *aliyah*, he is supposed to search for meaning or a special message for him in it. When something unusual or painful happens, we are enjoined to review our actions and see what might have been the catalyst for our deserving this tribulation.

In other words, we meet God all the time! There's always a reason, and always a place to turn for guidance and clarification. If we're on the wrong track, we can ask for help.

I remember a story I once heard, though some of the details escaped me so I made them up.

A man was walking through the forest, enjoying nature. "Ah, God," he said, "what a masterpiece You made in this world!" As he walked further he heard water rushing and, wishing to see more of God's handiwork, he headed towards the sound. "*Ribono shel Olam*," he cried when he came to the cliff from whence he could see the water rushing past hundreds of feet below, "I see Your signature in this place as clear as day."

Suddenly, he heard a noise behind him. He turned to see a huge bear rearing up and ready to run at him. With a bear on one side and a cliff on the other, he was out of options. "Hashem!" he called out. "I don't know what to do. Give me a sign!" There was a huge clap of thunder and suspended in mid-air over the river were four fiery letters. They read, "J-U-M-P."

"Lord," he called, "give me another sign!"

We are visited by Hashem all the time, and He gives us His calling card to let us know He was there. Sometimes, though, we are uncomfortable with the message, and so we chalk it up to happenstance and go about our merry way as if nothing happened.

That's when we're no different than the people who tell you you'll meet God when you die. You don't have to live with Him; you just have to die with Him. That was Bilaam's prayer after all, wasn't it? *"Tamos nafshi mos yesharim* — Let me die the death of the righteous" (*Bamidbar* 23:10). He wanted to die like a *tzaddik* as long as he didn't have to live like one.

Now, I'm not trying to scare anyone or make you depressed that you'll never be good enough. On the contrary, you're quite fortunate that *HaKadosh Baruch Hu* thinks you're important enough to send messages to. And if you think He doesn't think that, why do you think He arranged for you to read this article? Clearly He thinks highly of you. So what does He expect?

I think that like any other advertiser, He's happy if you get His messages even five percent of the time and recognize the value of His product. I think that when you see something unusual, or even something normal that catches your eye and makes you think, Hashem just wants you to take the time to ponder what He might have meant by it.

You don't have to be a prophet to get messages from God; you get them every day. Where the prophecy comes in is with the interpretation. *Nevi'im* didn't get words and phrases handed to them. They saw visions and interpreted the messages (with some help from Hashem, of course). We all see visions; we just may not recognize them for what they are. But, with a little practice, we can start to see the signs and get the messages Hashem is sending our way.

But in case you're out of practice, and it wasn't clear enough before, here's your sign:

ATTENTION DEAR READER:

I WILL BE TALKING TO YOU EVERY DAY. KEEP YOUR EYES AND EARS OPEN BECAUSE I WANT TO HAVE A MEANINGFUL CONVERSATION WITH YOU.

LOVE, GOD

Two Signs, One Message

*M*Y *FAITHFUL READERS WILL* remember that I see little notes and messages from Hashem at every turn. I think we all do, but perhaps I'm more tuned in to actually noticing and remembering them, possibly because I have so many readers whom I can inspire when I pick up on something.

One Shabbos, as I was *davening Minchah* in shul, something caught my eye. It was one of those folding, wooden, table-top *shtenders* that we all get for our budding young *talmidei chachamim*. Most of them have the prodigy's name painted on them, and an inspiring *pasuk*, like, "*V'hagisa ba yomam va'lailah* — You shall study [Torah] day and night."

What caught my eye was that this one was different. On the top it had the words, "*Mah ahavti Torasecha, kol hayom hi sichasi* — How I love your Torah, it's all I can talk about!" It struck me that this was a much more upbeat, feel-good message.

Instead of Torah being foisted on young people because they HAVE to toil in it around the clock (which is still an obligation, of course), this *shtender* inspires more learning because learning Torah makes *me* feel good and gives *me* purpose.

I have a marketing background and I can tell you that if you look at successful advertising, it's not geared to forcing anyone to do anything; rather, it hints in a subtle way that you might be allowed to join the elite ranks who know the sheer joy of driving a certain car... wearing a certain item of clothing/cosmetics...

9

traveling to… eating such wonderful food as… insert your item here.

Even things that are necessary are advertised in this way. For example, no diet plan ever advertises, "Fat people are unhealthy and die sooner — Join Weight Watchers today!" Nobody would do it because it frames it in negativity. Instead, they talk about feeling good about yourself, looking good, fitting into special clothes and getting compliments from others.

So why should it be, I wondered, as I noticed this differently worded *shtender,* that Torah should be pitched as something you *have* to do?

The same applies to Shabbos. The people who dread it as a day of "Don't do this" and "You can't do that" feel that way. That's because when they were growing up all they heard was "don't" and "you're not allowed to." What nobody ever said to them was, "It's special for Shabbos" or "Because it's Shabbos you get to eat extra sweets… stay up late…" Nobody helped them savor the experience of spending time with the family or singing *zemiros,* and they never heard anyone say, "It's so wonderful not to have to answer the phone or open bills" or "*Baruch Hashem*, it's Shabbos and we get a chance to stop running around!"

In fact, all of Judaism should be understood in that context. I can't tell you how many times I've been so glad to relinquish tough decisions because it was a clear *halachah.* "Do I say something about X, Y, and Z or not?" Well, *halachah* tells you what to say and how to say it.

The Torah tells us how to behave in order to get the maximum pleasure out of life, but nobody's telling it to these kids who grow up to be adults with an aversion to *Yiddishkeit, Rachmana litzlan.* We're not teaching them that it will make them feel good and happy to follow the Torah. It's like telling people, "If you don't use Colgate/Crest/Adwe plus Fluoride, you will lose all your teeth and will never be able to eat apples or popcorn!" A powerful argument, perhaps, but not one that will have them doing cartwheels to the bathroom sink.

Which brings me back to my message from Hashem. While I was musing over the *shtender*, thinking that it would make a good idea for an article, I saw another *shtender* on the next table with the original *pasuk* urging constant toil. Then I noticed the names on them and was stunned by the beauty and completeness of God's little lesson to me.

The name on the one *shtender*, which focused on Torah as an obligation to work, was Ari, "a lion." Lions are scary. They are the kings of the jungle because if you don't watch out they will eat you up. Not the most positive message for a young Torah student.

On the other *shtender*, where Hashem showed me the *pasuk* of how much the Torah makes its learners happy, was the name Baruch, "blessed."

The message screamed at me in its obvious simplicity. Two ways of conveying the same idea; one puts people off and the other draws them close. If we view Torah as a job, and present it to our children that way, it becomes a frightening monster. However, if we really recognize that it is good for us and makes us feel good, we will view the Torah and Judaism as it truly is: a special, valuable, wonderful *berachah*.

A Tree Grows in Brooklyn

R ECENTLY, I WAS LEARNING *Chovos HaLevavos* (I highly recommend it — a definite MUST-READ) and I got up to the Gate of Distinction, where one is urged to recognize the Almighty through His works, and specifically in nature. By seeing how He created the world, we can infer something about His wisdom and ability, and by noticing how things work, we can learn what purpose they serve.

Shortly thereafter, I was in Brooklyn for Shabbos. As I walked to shul Shabbos morning, I noticed something that is more common in Brooklyn than where I live in Monsey. A tree along the sidewalk had overgrown its postage stamp-sized grassy patch and the roots pushed up on the sidewalk, causing it to crack and crumble.

I suddenly remembered my *Chovos HaLevavos* training and tried to glean a lesson from that. I know that concrete is harder than wood, and yet the tree had forced its way through the sidewalk. I thought a little more deeply. It wasn't a question of wood versus concrete. How does a tree grow? Cells grow, fill with fluids and sap and extend the reach of the roots. (Okay botanists, I don't want any angry letters if I've done this wrong, this is just my impression.)

Basically, a teeny tiny shoot fills with water, grows, and eventually builds up the strength to smash concrete. I thought about that.

"*Ki ha-adam eitz ha-sadeh* — Man is a tree of the field." We are compared to trees, so obviously we can learn about our strengths from their strengths. I told myself: Hashem doesn't expect me to move mountains in an instant. Instead, what He wants is slow, consistent growth, making sure to imbibe plenty of water (a.k.a. Torah) and extend our reach. When we do that, any obstacles in our way will be eradicated.

A bit further, I noticed another tree. This one had a small white metal garden fence around it. At first it looked comical; that someone would put this teeny-tiny fence around this teeny tiny spot of land. But I thought about it; what could I learn from this?

I realized that a person can find beauty and contentment wherever he is willing to look for it. This homeowner felt that his tree was special and did his share to highlight and enhance it. He made the world just a touch more beautiful. Now, you might think that a rusting little fence might not be so attractive, but that's when you look at the externals of it. Then you see the fence and the rust spots and the cracked sidewalk. But if you look to the *penimius*, to the intentions behind the fence, that someone wanted to do something good and loving, then you see something that is truly very beautiful.

In *Pirkei Avos* (3:9) we are taught: "One who is learning on a journey, and interrupts his learning and says, 'How lovely is this tree' is nearly worthy of losing his life." The simple understanding is that he has interrupted his learning and for that he is deserving of punishment; he should have been more diligent.

However, I once heard a beautiful and thought-provoking explanation. The word for interrupt can also mean separate. If he is learning and notes the tree, that is not a problem. However, if he differentiates between his learning and Nature, he is denying the hand of Hashem in Creation and missing the point.

The Torah is the blueprint for the world, so wherever we look in the world, we should see Torah. When we see the tree break through the sidewalk, it should mean something to us. When we see the glory of a sunrise we should acknowledge Hashem's mastery of the world.

This lesson that I learned, and shared with you today, may not be the only reason, but I'm sure it is one of the reasons that a tree grows in Brooklyn.

That's the Ticket!

WHILE DRIVING HOME FROM a store very close to my home, I was too lazy to put on my seatbelt. My mind began to ramble to itself: "I'm really close, what's the big deal? Sure, they say most accidents happen within one mile of home, but that's at the end of a long trip where people let their guard down right? — What's that joke? Oh yeah, this guy heard most accidents happen within a mile of home — so he moved! My mother would want me to wear my seatbelt so it's *kibud eim....*"

None of these arguments really worked, but then I thought about the fact that sometimes local police hide in driveways and ticket people for not wearing their seatbelts. I reached over and put it on.

It's amazing if you think about it. Am I really more worried about a $100 fine than about my own life? Well, some sarcastic people may answer yes, but no rational person would really choose to die rather than pay some money. I think what it comes down to is just what we think the odds of something happening are. We don't think an accident will happen to us, but we do think it's likely that a cop might be lurking where we don't see him.

In other words, the likeliness of the event is what motivates us more than the more severe nature of it. Yes, death is somewhat more permanent than a fine or a point or two on your license, but the odds are against it, right?

What would happen if someone put on their seatbelt, or slowed their speed only because the cops were on the road, and then got into an accident where the belt or slower speed saved their lives? I'd venture to say they'd be so thankful for the policemen on the road that they'd begin to consider those men in blue a welcome sight.

At *Matan Torah*, Hashem held *Har Sinai* over our heads and said, "If you keep the Torah, good. If not, there shall be your burial place," indicating that He would drop the mountain on us. It was a threat, not veiled in any way, and quite clear. I remember a fellow once saying to me: "I disagree with that. That's not how you speak to people."

I was speechless because I didn't think I needed to defend God. I mean, He's God! He can do what He wants. Want proof? Look at the platypus: It's a mammal, but it lays eggs. It looks like a beaver, but has a duck's bill. What would Darwin have to say about that?

So, if Hashem speaks to people "that way," that's okay by me. Now, to be fair, the fellow wasn't necessarily arguing with Hashem's decision, but rather with the rabbi in the Gemara who said that it happened that way. I don't think I'd want to start up with a rabbi of that caliber either, but what the man probably meant to impart was, "I know that the way to motivate people is by being positive, not threatening to break their noses. That's not how you get them to listen. You've got to make them realize why it's better for them to do what the Torah says." He more likely disagreed with the general approach, not the actual fact.

Whether or not that is the case I can't say, but it definitely makes sense. Why, then, would Hashem hold the mountain over us and threaten to drop it if He could have motivated us in a more positive, loving way?

Let's go back to my seatbelt reverie. I think that if I drive safely, I won't need my seatbelt because I won't have an accident. That doesn't mean the cop won't see me safely driving along on my merry way and not give me a ticket. Even if I tell him I live close by and I justify my actions, he can throw the book at me because the law doesn't recognize my rationales. Therefore, I put on my seatbelt not because I think I will have an accident, but because I don't want to get hit with a fine.

When Hashem gave us the Torah, He told us to keep it and live by it. That's like us driving merrily along. Then He held the mountain over us — that's the cop.

If we were just told how wonderful it is to live by the Torah, we could give ourselves excuses. We could rationalize that it's just a little white lie, or that we cheated just this one time, and so on. "I'm a good person," is a refrain we've all heard or said at one time or another, and we believe it to be true. However, being a "good person" is not the same as being a "good Jew."

More than that, many of us who would classify ourselves as "good Jews" might not be such "good Jews" according to the book the Cop is looking at. We might think we're proceeding safely, but we could be very wrong. It's the threat that Hashem might disagree with our position, despite the fact that we can rationalize and explain our actions, which scares us.

If Hashem isn't happy with me, He will punish me and I won't do well in business, or I'll have a problem finding a spouse. Although we often attribute our successes to our own skill and prowess, we find it easy to blame God when we don't do well, so this is a more believable outcome to us, like the policeman hiding in the bushes. When we get a ticket, it's not necessarily because we did something wrong, but because the cop had a quota to fill. We never actually think about the death part of it, because we don't think that will ever happen (a genetic throwback to Adam who was supposed to live forever).

In other words, what keeps us on the straight and narrow sometimes is not the more severe threat, but the more benign one, which we can imagine happening more readily. In that case, when

Hashem held the mountain over us and threatened us, he did us a huge favor.

Just as the specter of a ticket which made us put on our belts or slow down might save our lives, the threat of Hashem punishing us can be more effective at keeping us on the path of good fortune and success than all the promises of wonderful reward!

So, the next time you have a chance on the road of life to play by the rules and be a model citizen, remember that it may not only save your life, but also your soul.

Someday You'll Understand

M Y FATHER OFTEN MENTIONED the impasse he reached when talking to his father. "You'll understand when you're a father," he was told. "So I became a father, and then he said, 'You'll understand when you're a grandfather.' When I became a grand-father, he became a great-grandfather, I can never catch up!"

It may be true that we can't understand what our parents feel until we experience it for ourselves, and that may take some time. However, Hashem is neither a grandfather nor a great-grandfather. He is everyone's Father, which means we have the opportunity to catch a glimpse of what He feels when we are parents. That means we're hopefully not so set in our ways that we can't learn and change from our experiences.

The other day I had what I like to call a "God moment." It's when we get a glimpse of His perspective in the world. I once wrote about an experience wherein I knew I intended to give someone money and he felt that he only got it because he got up and walked over to ask me.

This time, I was walking my daughter to the bus one rainy morning. She had a small umbrella with her, and I was walking just behind her with my large golf umbrella, holding it not only over myself but also over her, as I knew her umbrella would not suffice.

I thought to myself, "She thinks she's dry because she's hold-ing an umbrella. She doesn't even realize that she's staying dry because I am holding *my* umbrella over hers!" I realized that so often we think we're doing things, protecting ourselves, and we are completely unaware that Hashem is guiding and guarding us. (Of course, it didn't hit me until later that when I thought I was protecting her with my umbrella, it was really Hashem protecting her by sending me to do it, and He was guiding the rain and my umbrella so I didn't get a single drop more on me than I was supposed to either.)

By realizing that Hashem is our Father, we can extrapolate other things. We tell our children what to do not because we want them to suffer, but because we, through our knowledge and experience, understand how things work.

We know that a child's idea of a balanced meal is a lollipop in each hand. Our ideas of what is healthy and beneficial are quite different, even if the children don't see it that way now. Inevitably, though, they grow out of it and when they become parents themselves, they understand too.

If we use that concept and apply it to Hashem, life becomes much easier. Right now, there are many things that seem sweet and pleasurable to us, but Hashem says we can't have them or do them. We may scream and have a tantrum about how it's not fair (a concept that doesn't exist in Judaism — and note that it is common for Israelis to say, "*zeh lo* fair!") but Father knows best and He understands how the world works.

One of the best speeches I ever heard likened the Torah to an instruction manual for the world. A banana has a built-in gauge for ripeness. If it's yellow it's good, if it's green it's not yet ripe. Nobody will stop you from eating a green banana, but if you do you will get sick.

The Torah tells you what is good for your soul and what is bad for your soul. Nobody will stop you from speaking *lashon hara* or lying or eating the candy with the questionable *hashgachah*, but if you do, you will get sick.

If we remember that Hashem is our Father Who loves us and TRULY knows what's best for us, then life's medicines don't have to be so bitter or hard to swallow. On top of that, if my interaction with my own kids is any guide, if we take it with a smile, the odds are we'll get a reward right away just for the way in which we took it, aside from the long-term benefits.

I think I'm beginning to understand. Sweet!

I Hear Dead People

I'VE NEVER BEEN A fan of scary stories or haunted houses, and I doubt that most of our readership has ever thought about whether ghosts exist or not. They probably do, but we'd call them any number of other names: *sheidim, dybbuks, neshamos,* and so on. We know that there is life after death, so the thought doesn't surprise us that someone might hear from a person who has left this earth.

What I want to speak about this time is an experience I had one Shabbos morning. I had woken up for some inexplicable reason at 5:30 A.M. Being that *Shacharis* was not until 8:45, I thought I might go back to sleep. And then I heard it.

It was a disembodied voice that said, "Who am I, Pharaoh?" I recognized that voice.

When I was a *bachur* in yeshivah, one of the older yeshivah students was Menachem Kohn *z"l*, affectionately known as Mikey. Later, he was one of the *kollel* fellows in the Telz *Kollel*. One day, as I passed him in the *beis midrash* just before *seder*, he was telling someone how he had woken up at 5 A.M. (or some other such ridiculously early time) and decided to learn. I interjected and asked why he didn't go back to sleep.

"Go back to sleep? Who am I, Pharaoh?" referring to the fact that Pharaoh had a dream that woke him up, but immediately he was back asleep and dreaming. It stuck with me.

Mikey was killed last year in the Catskills as he was preparing to bring his family home to Cleveland at the end of the summer. He may be gone physically, but he's still here in spirit.

Over the years, I have heard that voice when I've woken up early. Sometimes it works, sometimes it doesn't. Lately, though, when I hear those words in my head and remember Mikey's expression of shock that someone would roll over and go back to sleep, I get up to learn. That's what happened that Shabbos morning, and on a Sunday morning, and a couple of days in between over the past few weeks when I've awoken earlier than I had planned.

It's not surprising that I hear dead people. I still hear the voice of my *rosh yeshivah*, R' Gifter *z"l*, as he roared, "A Jew never walks alone!" when I offered to accompany him. I hear other voices, too.

We all do. We have experiences and people who've made a difference in our lives. We have stray memories that stick with us and we don't know why. We have to keep looking back and finding the message.

It also means that other people hear us too. They remember something we've said, or done, or how we made them feel for a moment in time. That's a big responsibility, and a great opportunity.

Tzaddikim are considered alive even after death because they still speak to us. Who hasn't had a conversation with Rashi or the Ohr HaChaim or the Vilna Gaon? We are inspired by their words, their stories, the way they made us feel.

We can have that effect on others too, for who knows what people will remember? That's why it is so important to try to be a positive influence on others. They will hear us long after we're gone.

One last thing, for the people who like the spooky stuff...

That morning, when I heard Mikey say, "Who am I, Pharaoh?" and it made me get out of bed and learn? That day was *chof zayin Menachem Av*, Mikey's first *yahrtzeit*.

Epilogue: After I submitted this article, I mentioned the story to a friend from my yeshivah days. He related a similar incident. A boy from our yeshivah was going to Eretz Yisrael to learn. Before the bachur left, my friend said to him, "You know, Eretz Yisrael is a great opportunity for you. It's a new place, and since you're a Kohen, you'll get the opportunity to duchen (recite Birchas Kohanim) every day."

It is ten years later, and that bachur is married and still learning in Israel. About two years ago, he told my friend how he still remembered those words, and though his attendance at Shacharis in America had been spotty at best, from the time he had arrived in Eretz Yisrael, he davened with a minyan regularly. My friend was just trying to give him some encouragement. Who would have imagined it would change his life?

Marketing and Stuff

I AM WRITING THIS ARTICLE at the Tire Center at Costco. Not one to waste time, I brought my laptop so you could all join me for the thrilling experience of waiting for my car to be ready. As I walked in, I had to smile at the sign I passed. On the front of the store is a sign with an arrow pointing to the spot where I now stand. It reads, "For your convenience, tires are sold in the Tire Center." That's great! So much more convenient than when tires used to be sold in the produce aisle.

I know what they were trying to say, but it's a great segue into this article's topic — Marketing. In specific, what is important to people and makes them buy a particular product. In my magazine column, I have written about the history of Coca Cola. Here, I'd like to talk about Pepsi.

Not the history of Pepsi, nor even the history of any particular era. Today, I'd like to focus on one particular ad campaign they ran when I was in yeshivah, and which they have revived to some degree. The slogan, as I recall, which would entice you to envision yourself guzzling an ice-cold Pepsi, with the cool droplets of water dripping off it in the hot summer sun, feeling the utmost refreshment, actually conveyed none of that delicious imagery. No, the slogan they used to sell Pepsi was:

Drink Pepsi. Get stuff.

That's it. "Drink Pepsi. Get stuff." Nothing else. After that there was presumably a catalog where you could trade in points or bottle caps for such wondrous items as T-shirts, pens, Frisbees and can holders. Now, as a *bachur* in yeshivah, perhaps already exercising my comedic skills, I envisioned the marketing geniuses who came up with that slogan.

"Dude, how can we get people to drink more Pepsi?"

"I dunno man. That's a tough one."

"Wait a minute, I got it! We can give them stuff!"

"Sure! Uh… like what should we give them?"

"I dunno, like, stuff."

"Excellent!"

And just like that, these two boneheads were probably getting paid $100,000 a year (a lot of money when I was in yeshivah) to come up with this brilliant plan. But you know what's even scarier? It was successful! That's right, people bought Pepsi not because it tasted good, not because they liked it, but to get something. What were they trying to get? STUFF!

I think it says a lot about our society when we become focused on materialism to the point where we don't even care what we're getting, as long as we're getting something. The truth is, when you wear a Pepsi T-shirt, you just become a walking billboard for them, yet we wear commercial logos like a trophy, as if they were sponsoring our run to catch the bus or our attempt at a slam dunk in the bungalow colony basketball game. (Anyone who knows me will find that last image even more hilarious.)

But, if we get something, we're willing to spend more for it, as long as we feel like we're getting it for free. How many of us have spent thirty dollars to "win" a stuffed animal at a carnival or amusement park? How about racking up a twenty-dollar tab on tokens and skeeball to get enough tickets to trade in for a 14-cent plastic necklace?

The truth is, it's human nature to want things and to do crazy things to get them. That's where the genius of the Pepsi campaign shines through. They knew that people would buy their drink not because of its merits or virtues, but because of their selfishness. However, there is an antidote. It's called Torah.

There's an old joke about when Hashem went around to various nations offering them the Torah. He went to one nation and said, "Would you like my Torah?"

"What's in it?" they asked.

"Well," said God, "It says things like 'Don't kill.'"

"No thanks," came the reply.

The next group — "Want My mitzvos?"

"What are they?"

"Don't steal."

"Sorry, not interested."

Finally Hashem came to Moshe. "Do you want My commandments?" asked the Master of the World.

"How much do they cost?" asked Moshe.

"Why, they're free, of course."

"Good, I'll take ten."

It's sad because that's really how people think of the Jewish people, focused on money. It's sadder that for many it is true. But the end of the story doesn't have to be that way.

The Torah teaches us to value other things. It teaches us to be happy with what we have because we realize that Hashem is like a doctor, giving us the exact dosage of success that we need to be healthy. If we push and insist on taking extra doses against doctor's orders, He won't stop us, but we will get sick.

Torah teaches us that the things that are really valuable are the mitzvos, the people in our lives, improving ourselves, and getting to know *HaKadosh Baruch Hu*. Those are the things money can't buy. And they're much more valuable than anything Pepsi is giving out.

One more thing, this campaign is not original to Pepsi. If you look in *Parshas Bechukosai*, Hashem said, "If you keep My laws, I will give you rain at its proper time, and the land will produce much. There will be peace in the land and you will have more food than you can eat. I will dwell with you and make you My people."

If I had to summarize this promise of Hashem?

Live Torah. Get *lots* of stuff.

Now THAT'S excellent.

And Now a Word from Our Sponsor

*A*DVERTISING IS EVERYWHERE. It almost seems to be a nuisance. No matter where you go, someone is trying to sell you something. Wouldn't it be nice if there were no ads in the world?

Now, before you answer that, let's think about it. Say you want to turn on the radio to hear the traffic. (I mean, why else would you turn off the *shiur* you were listening to in the car? To hear some political mouthpiece spout his opinions, which have no effect anyway?!) You may say that those annoying commercials are standing in the way of you hearing what you need, but think again. If not for those advertising dollars, there would be no radio broadcast whatsoever. Forget the traffic, you wouldn't hear anything.

Think about this the next time you pick up a magazine. Without advertising, it wouldn't only be lighter, it would be gone. You see, the ads are what make any media able to continue. So what's that got to do with you? A lot.

First off, as we've discussed before, it's very important to make people feel good. When someone buys something, you're supposed to praise it, making them feel good about their decision. Well, here's a great chance. Think about it. Someone advertises in a magazine and doesn't know if people saw their ad. If you walk in and say, "Hey, I saw your ad in...," they will be very happy. Not only have you made their day, you've ensured yourself

29

continued support of the wonderful publication you enjoy.

So, if you take the time out to call a couple of stores, and say, "I saw your ad and the next time I need [fill in the blank] I will think of you," [something I highly recommend you do] you're doing a great mitzvah of being *meshabe'ach mekcho* (praising someone's purchase) and making *them* feel good, plus you're helping enable yourself to continue to read such wondrous prose as my mental meanderings in my magazine columns. But I'm not here to simply talk about advertising.

Everything in the world has a spiritual counterpart and this topic is no exception. R' Paysach Krohn tells a great *mashal* in the name of Rabbi Dwek about a man from the backwoods who came into town to mail a letter.

The postmaster told him, "You can't mail this letter, it's too heavy. You need to add three more stamps."

"Add more stamps?!" asked the country bumpkin incredulously, "but then it will be even heavier!"

The foolish man didn't realize that yes, it would make it heavier, but that's what would enable the letter to be delivered. The same is true, Rabbi Dwek explained, with *tzedakah*. The Gemara in *Gittin* (7a) says, "If one feels his financial resources are strained, he should give *tzedakah* from them (and certainly if his finances are abundant.)" What? Give away his money when he doesn't have enough? Then he'll be even more strained!

Not at all — because it's the *tzedakah* that's going to carry him through and enable the flow of *parnasah* to continue. Much like the advertising that permits the radio broadcast, the money spent on others enables you to enjoy a sufficient livelihood yourself.

Want another important commercial in your life? How about reflecting on your Personal Sponsor? If we use the parable of the radio station: Who enables you to function, to achieve, to broadcast what you have to offer, and enjoy the fruits of your labors? Isn't it Hashem?

In other words, *HaKadosh Baruch Hu* is one big sponsor, paying and flowing the resources through to us so that we might continue to exist. It would only be right that we call Him and say, "I saw Your ad in my body today. It was really moving," or "I caught Your lightshow at dawn — it was awesome!"

Well, as a matter of fact, we do. *Modeh Ani* is a commercial break acknowledging that Hashem gave us back our souls. *Asher Yatzar* is another fine example. We thank Hashem for giving us the ability to function and for creating the wonderful workings of our bodies. We shouldn't look at it as some obligatory *berachah* which we "have to say," but as an opportunity to encourage our Sponsor to continue His advertising, knowing that it works. When we recognize the Creator, we're giving Him a reason to continue to support us and ultimately, we're the beneficiaries.

Did you ever get a cut? I did. As I write this, I am looking at a cut on my finger which was very deep and painful just two weeks ago. Now, it's almost gone and will soon look as if it never existed. Several times during the healing process I have marveled at the *Ribono shel Olam*'s kindness in giving us a body which heals itself. R' Avigdor Miller *z"l* points out that no other tool gets tougher as you use it, but the human hand does. If one works hard with it, the skin gets thicker to protect us. Unbelievable! Thanks, Hashem! Mankind hasn't come up with a better product and they likely never will.

We go through *Shemoneh Esreh* and thank our Sponsor for all His wonderful products: intelligence, forgiveness, health, *parnasah*, Justice, accepting *tefillah* and so on. Hey, why stop at one? Collect the whole set!

From time to time, it behooves us to thank Hashem and acknowledge the things we take for granted. The ability to use a computer, to type, to see. I was thinking about it on my way to shul this morning. Have you ever tried to stand on a surfboard or raft in the water? Did you feel secure? I didn't think so.

Now, when you say the *berachah*, "*Roka ha'aretz al ha-mayim* — Who established and firmed the land over the water," aren't you thanking Hashem that the streets you walk on don't shimmy and slide out from under you like that tremulous raft? I'd say that's a product I'm happy to endorse.

So, every day, while you're enjoying the broadcast of kindness from Hashem, take time out to acknowledge the Sponsor. It will ensure years of healthy, happy, uninterrupted programming.

Look on the Bright Side

HAVING ESTABLISHED THAT WE are in communication with the Almighty on a constant basis, we should be more able to see that the things that seem daunting, harmful, or just downright bad are not as they seem.

Judaism offers us the hope born of understanding that Hashem is a permanent fixture in our lives. Since all He does is for our benefit and good, the things we experience have an aspect to them that we may have overlooked in our zeal to feel sorry for ourselves.

If God Is Your Co-Pilot, Switch Seats

W*HEN SITTING IN TRAFFIC,* or waiting in line at the grocery store, I often tell myself that it is God Who decides how quickly or slowly I will move, and how long I will wait. That helps to alleviate the stress somewhat when the idiot in the car in front of me puts his right blinker on at every street for two miles, hesitates as if contemplating a turn, then continues on before ultimately turning left without signaling.

I often cajole myself by thinking, "Maybe there's a cop waiting there and I might get a ticket," or "*Baruch Hashem*, perhaps if I had been at that spot a minute sooner I would have had an accident — this guy was sent to save me from that." It works sometimes, but you have to keep telling yourself that traffic is ordained from Heaven like everything else.

This week, I was rushing home from work when a large utility truck pulled in front of me. He was going slowly and I couldn't see anything ahead of him, so I made a decision. I had an option to go straight or turn right at the next intersection. Whichever he did, I would do the opposite. Of course, this flies in the face of my whole "pre-ordained" mantra, but I figured I could make my *hishtadlus*, right?

Anyway, I didn't have to make the decision as just before the intersection the utility truck turned into the school on the corner.

Baruch Hashem! Free of that guy at last! I continued on and made my right turn.

As I rounded the corner, the utility truck exited the school through its other driveway, and swung into place just ahead of me. The irony of the situation struck me and I burst out laughing. "*Ribono shel Olam*, that is great. You got me." There was no way I was going to get away from this truck. I thought I had it all planned out and Hashem said, "Ahem… I don't think so!" As I followed behind the truck, I reflected on this open display of Hashem's control of the world, and the message He was sending me about how much control I really have.

I realized I now had a theme for my Observant Jew article. But there was a problem. The truck stayed in front of me. What was that about? As we made the next turn (together of course) I saw the truck swerve a little, as if to avoid a pothole or small woodland creature (we have many of those in Monsey). Instinctively, I swerved too. Then I realized that I had seen nothing to cause me to swerve, I just did it because the truck did. I think that's when I got the second part of the message.

In life, like when we've got a big lumbering truck ahead of us, we can't see what's ahead and don't know how to plan for the future. We take our cues from the world around us and try to be prepared for anything. But ultimately, Hashem is the One deciding how much we will see and how far we will get. If we have to swerve, He sends us something to make us swerve. If we are not supposed to get where we want to as fast as we want to, we won't.

Often we forget this. We ask Hashem to give us things, thinking they will make us happy. We say "*Pose'ach es yadecha u'masbia l'chol chai ratzon* — You open Your hand and grant all life its desires," and expect Hashem to give us whatever we ask for. We forget that the next *pasuk* is, "*Tzaddik Hashem b'chol derachav* — God is righteous in all his ways." We have to realize that when it's not good for us, we won't get it. If it is good for us, nothing and nobody can deflect or hold it back from us.

I often get annoyed when I hear people discussing politics. "The President needs to do such-and-such," "Israel should just…" as if they have a clue about what is supposed to happen. I remember seeing that the reason whichever nation subjugates *Klal Yisrael* becomes a superpower is because then the leader's actions are established by *HaKadosh Baruch Hu,* as the *pasuk* says, "The heart of kings and princes are in Hashem's hand." That means that every action that takes place on the world stage is directed by the *Ribono shel Olam.* We can't dictate what needs to happen; we can just play our parts to the best of our ability.

So, the next time you're tempted to pontificate about world events (other than to initiate *Tehillim* or learning as a *zechus*) or you're thinking about racing to the fast-moving line at Wal-Mart (ok, let's call it poetic license — there's really no such thing), remember that Hashem is directing your movements and those of the players around you. Then just smile, it's time for your close-up.

Murphy's Law vs Torah Law

*A*FTER RETURNING FROM A short vacation and a long flight (or as they say, it wasn't a vacation, it was a family trip…), I proceeded to unpack the car and bring in the suitcases. In one of my multiple trips, I shlepped a large suitcase upstairs to be unpacked by my wife. "You remembered to leave the suitcase with laundry in it downstairs in the laundry room, right?" she asked me. I didn't even have to open it — I knew.

Although the technical odds of my having brought up the suitcase with items to be unpacked and leaving the one with laundry downstairs was 50/50, I knew with near certainty that the bag I had lugged up the stairs was the laundry which I would now have to lug downstairs, and bring up the other one in its place.

Why should that be? Two words — Murphy's Law. Nearly everyone is familiar with Murphy's Law, though its history is somewhat vague. It is most commonly attributed to a military engineer named Edward Murphy who had designed a rocket sled for the U.S. military which failed to perform on its testing day in 1948 because every single sensor had been wired incorrectly. His remarks at the time have been boiled down to the familiar, "Anything that can go wrong, will go wrong."

So, with a nod to Colonel Murphy, I opened the bag to discover that yes, indeed, I had brought up the laundry-filled suitcase and would be getting some extra exercise. Then I thought about it. How did I know with such certainty that it would be that way?

Is it simple pessimism? What about the *Ribono shel Olam*? Since He runs the world, why does He let Murphy have his way all the time?

Having a good yeshivah background, with a solid fifteen minutes of *mussar seder* each day, and a solid one or two days a year that I utilized it, I came up with the answer — *yissurim shel ahavah*! That must be it. Murphy's Law was originated simply to explain the fact that Hashem often takes the opportunity to give us a little nudge by having the worse of two scenarios take place in what are most often inconsequential events in the grand scheme of things.

Take this case of Murphy's Law for example: "A slice of buttered bread, when dropped, will always land butter-side down." An alternate version of that is: "The probability of a slice of buttered bread falling butter-side down is directly proportional to the price of carpet."

In both cases, something bad happened. You were prepared to eat a nice buttered sandwich, when you somehow dropped it. It fell buttered side down, which means that all the shmutz from the floor will now be on your bread, and you will have to take another slice and go through the trouble of buttering it. Wow, what a pain.

Or, it falls on the carpet. Now you have a stained carpet that you must carefully clean. A bit more trouble, but much less difficult than, say, having a tire blowout while driving 175MPH on the Autobahn in a borrowed Porsche.

In essence, Murphy's Law highlights the kindness of Hashem Who gives us suffering in insignificant ways (like reaching into your pocket for a quarter and pulling out a nickel), thereby lessening the really traumatic suffering we might otherwise have to endure.

Speaking of enduring, why has Murphy's Law gained such permanence in our minds and our lexicon? What makes it so special that it stands out? When I gave it a bit of thought, I realized that the Gemara in *Berachos* gives us our answer. In *Berachos* 5a, the Gemara discusses *yissurin*, suffering that Hashem sends to people. One dictum states, "Whoever has the opportunity to learn Torah but does not, Hashem brings terrible *yissurin* upon him."

I started thinking, what does the name Murphy sound like? "*Me'rafui*" — which means "from weakness," as it says that *B'nei Yisrael* left Refidim, where "*Rafu yadeihem mi'divrei Torah* — their hands were weakened in learning Torah." Murphy — *Me'rafui*, I think it's too close to be a coincidence, if those exist anyway.

Murphy's actual law, then, is that "Anything that can go wrong, will… unless you are doing everything right!"

But we can find an even better message if we look to the purpose of Murphy's Law as it was intended to be. Most people take it at face value, that it was merely an expression of pessimism. However, in truth, Murphy's Law embodies the concept of "defensive design" — anticipating the mistakes the end-user is likely to make.

His sensors failed because there were two ways to connect them. One would give accurate readings; one would just make a mess. His assistant chose the wrong one and caused the failure. The message, therefore, is that one must anticipate the pitfalls and avoid a scenario where there are two such diverse options.

We are constantly faced with choices between good and bad, right and wrong. However, if we are wired so that we can only perform one way, we might avoid the mistakes and save ourselves a lot of aggravation.

You see, Murphy WAS an optimist. He wasn't complaining about things going wrong, he was commenting on how we can get them to go right.

So, after I finished reflecting on this, and how suffering is just God's way of reminding you to learn and do mitzvos, I went to the bookshelf, got a Gemara, and sat down to learn. Hey, I can take a hint, can't you?

Negativity Stinks!
(or: My Life As a Pollyanna)

I hate negative people. These are the folks who believe that every silver lining has a cloud and they are constantly griping about something or someone. They are such a waste of oxygen! No matter what happens, they make some sarcastic, rotten comment. What awful human beings.

You could say the most innocuous comment to them but they will take it as an insult because they are so self-centered and enjoy "suffering" so much that they will automatically assume you're out to get them. If someone makes a mistake, they will ridicule that person to no end, harping on their foolishness. These caustic people are just plain mean and it would be great if they just dropped dead.

Whew! Forget it, I can't write like that anymore. I was trying to prove a point by trying to be one of "them" but I can't do it. Unfortunately, there are people out there who we run into every day who enjoy complaining and, for some odd reason, they think it will win them friends. They think people look up to them when they're putting people down, instead of recognizing the inevitable fact that it will cause them loneliness.

Nobody likes to be around a bitter person, and yet, people persist in their cynicism. A pessimist will often say, "I'm not a pessimist, I'm a realist. I'm just stating the facts as they really are."

The truth is, the facts usually aren't completely apparent, so they're just stating the facts "as they appear to them." Interestingly enough, reality is often as subjective as perception is and is created by how we perceive things. How so? Let me explain.

Let's say that someone said something to you which could be taken in one of two ways. If you take it as a negative comment, you are creating the fact that there is now animosity between the two of you. You're also creating a feeling of hurt within yourself that you blame the other person for.

However, if you chose instead to take the comment as positive, or impartial, you would not feel bad, and the next time you saw them you might be friendly and have a good time. Now, the fact that this is the *halachah* is just gravy. If you were an optimist, you wouldn't get an upset stomach because someone harmed you, and because of that, they wouldn't have. In other circumstances, when someone was insensitive to me, I'd rather believe they were careless than that they were maliciously out to get me. If I choose to believe the negative about their act, am I stating the facts as they are, or creating a reality based on my feeling?

If it's the latter (and it is), then that means I can control my own reality. I once saw a great T-shirt that said, "I reject your reality and substitute it with my own." I love that because it's truer than we often care to admit.

There was a newspaper article about "High Holiday Jews" using their Blackberries and PDA's outside of Temple on Rosh Hashanah [Note: THEY WOULD NEVER DREAM OF DOING IT INSIDE.] I heard numerous comments on that. Some people were blasting these people who obviously hadn't had a similar upbringing and equating them with non-Jews. Others were defending them and reminding others that they are our Jewish brothers and sisters even if their deeds don't match identically to ours.

I was disgusted that so many made it a point to condemn them. On Rosh Hashanah, we quoted the curse/blessing of Bilaam which says, "*Lo hibit aven b'Yaakov, v'lo ra'ah amal b'Yisrael.*" It means that Hashem did not discern failings in the Jewish people. That doesn't mean they didn't exist, or that we are blameless, but that Hashem chooses to overlook our flaws out of His love for us.

Does that mean Hashem is out of touch with reality, *chas v'shalom*? On the contrary, Hashem IS reality. What that means to me is that we don't *have* to find things wrong with others, and we *should* try to see the best in people. That's how we can emulate *HaKadosh Baruch Hu* and be happier ourselves.

I've often been called a Pollyanna. Not knowing what that meant, I researched it. It comes from a fictional novel written in 1913 and a number of books about an orphan girl (Pollyanna) who goes through life playing "the Glad Game." In each situation, she finds the thing to be glad about. It started when she hoped to get a doll from a community donation box but all that was left was a pair of crutches. Her father had said, "Let's be glad we don't need them!"

In that case, I could be called a "Nachum" because, as we all know, the true story of Nachum Ish Gamzu far predates the Pollyanna books. He was called Ish Gamzu because no matter what happened, he said, "*Gam zu l'tovah* — This too is for the good."

In most situations, you don't have to find the truth, you just have to find an acceptable possible explanation, and you can go on merrily. If someone is mean, you can feel sorry for him because he's so bitter he probably feels he's been hurt. If something "bad" happens to you, you can try to figure out why it's good, because if Hashem made it happen, it must be good.

Even those pessimists serve a purpose and they are not, *chas v'shalom*, a waste of oxygen. If they're here, God has a good reason for it. So instead of looking for the negative points, we should look for the positive attributes of others. There's an old expression: "If you can't say something nice, don't say anything at all." I guess that works for a start, but to really experience happiness and enjoy life, staying silent isn't enough.

Instead, I prefer the adage, "If you can't say something nice, you're not trying hard enough." It can be done — I'm positive!

The Problem with Assuming

MAKING ASSUMPTIONS IS OFTEN a bad thing. In fact, one should almost never assume, and I assume you know why. No, I don't mean because there is an etymological insult in it. See, you assumed you knew the reason. No, the reason not to assume is because most of the time we assume wrong.

When we size up a situation quickly and decide that we know what's happening even though we don't have all the facts, we are taking a pretty big risk, and also, we might be committing a serious transgression. At the very least, we could come off looking ignorant, petty, or just plain foolish.

Let me give you an example. When I was in high school, one of the *bachurim* would make *havdalah* in the *beis midrash* on *motza'ei Shabbos*. One night, when I walked to the back room where the *havdalah* set was kept, I heard Ami, the boy who made *havdalah*, asking another boy to take the silver cup to the water fountain and put a little water in it.

I was proud of myself for knowing his reasoning. Of course, "*kos shel berachah tzarich shtifah v'hadachah*" (the cup to be used for *Kiddush*, *bentshing*, or the like needs to be cleaned prior to use). Some have the custom of making sure the cup is still wet. I assumed that was Ami's reasoning.

That's why when the younger boy brought back the *becher* with an inch of water in it, I took it from him, chuckled at his ignorance and flung most of it out into the garbage can, leaving just a few droplets of moisture. Ami jumped and emitted a gurgling sound that I presume was some amazing self-control on his part, then said in stilted tones: "I... needed... the water... because we don't have enough grape juice." Oops. I felt like an... well, I felt stupid.

You see, with my assumption, not only was I embarrassed, but I made someone else do more work, negated the work a third person had done, and overall made a bad decision.

How about another anecdote? Recently, I went to a bar mitzvah. It was a lovely affair, but what happened afterwards was quite unpleasant. We stayed for the *Kiddush* and then after lunch I put my *tallis* back on to wear it home. As I stood waiting for my wife, a fellow walked past me and on his way made a loud comment. With a sneer and a "Give me a break," look on his face, he said, "The *eruv* is just fine! You can carry your *tallis* home!"

It was clear that he was feeling insecure in his own religious observance and felt that by my wearing my *tallis*, I was making a statement that he, and the other "sinners" who use the *eruv*, were less *frum* than I. He assumed he knew the facts, but, as usual, he ended up looking foolish.

If he would have stopped to look before judging, he would have seen that I was carrying my *siddur* and a bag with my wife's shoes. "I use the *eruv*," I said, as he brushed past me with animosity, "I'm wearing my *tallis* because my Rabbi told me carrying it home would be *hachanah*, preparation from Shabbos for after Shabbos," a prohibited use. I don't think he heard me.

The point is, when he assumed he knew my reasons for wearing my *tallis* he made an accusation that was unfounded and ridiculous based on the facts. He assumed that the only reason not to carry my *tallis* was because of the *eruv*, forgetting (or maybe not knowing) that some *poskim* say you can't carry your *tallis* home because it looks like you're preparing for after Shabbos.

I was upset by the incident, as no one ever likes being accused unjustly, but the real loser was the fellow who made the assumption. To be honest, I don't think I even got a good look at his face so the only person who knows who it was is the guy himself. I'm just mentioning that so nobody assumes I'm looking for revenge (which would be another *issur*).

So by now, you probably figure it's safe to assume that one should never assume. Wrong again! Assuming serves an important function.

We are commanded to judge everyone favorably. That means assuming the best about them, even when we don't have all the facts. Not only that, we aren't supposed to look for the facts in that case.

Let's say someone insults you or slights you. You should assume that it was not done maliciously, and that they had no intention of hurting you. I know someone who doesn't speak to his cousin because thirty-five years ago, when he had a flat tire, his cousin drove right past and pretended like he didn't see him. He's assuming his cousin really did see him, and therefore he's been dragging this animosity around like an anvil around his neck for all this time.

If he had assumed that his cousin was preoccupied and didn't see him, and that if he had, not only would he have stopped but he would have fixed the tire himself *and* brought him a cup of coffee and a Danish while he waited, he would be a happier person and would not harbor bad feelings toward his cousin. He also would not have violated so many commandments about bearing grudges and hating people.

If you see someone walking into an establishment with a questionable *hashgachah*, you're supposed to assume he's going to use the bathroom, buy a soda, or, if you see him taking a bite of food, that he's under the impression that this *hechsher* is reputable. You should *not* assume that he has no regard for Torah and *halachah*.

In most cases, when we do find out the facts, we learn that people really are better than we give them credit for and most people *don't* want to hurt others or do something bad. They're most often *not* trying to insult you or your beliefs. (If you think I'm wrong, read my article — "Negativity Stinks! [or: My Life As a Pollyanna]" on page 41.)

We must stop and think about it, especially during the weeks leading up to the *Yamim Nora'im* when God will be judging us. We might assume that He would never assume, especially since He has all the facts. But, we'd be wrong.

You see, Hashem does judge with *mishpat*, but he also judges *middah k'neged middah* (measure for measure). In other words, if we look at someone's actions and decide that there is a reasonable, justifiable explanation for what he's doing that looks wrong, Hashem will do the same for us.

If we feel that we don't need all the facts to come to a favorable conclusion, Hashem may take the same path in His judgment of us, and perhaps ignore some of the Prosecutor's juicier details and find us worthy of being inscribed and sealed for a happy and sweet new year.

That's My Job

THREE MEN WERE SITTING around a table. "*Oooooyyyyyy*," sighed the first. "*Ooooyyyy veeeeyyy*," *krechtzed* the second. Whereupon the third said, "Hey, I thought we agreed not to talk about work!"

When it comes to work, people often look at it as a necessary evil, something to be done under duress like death and taxes. However, it really doesn't have to be that way, and an attitude adjustment just might make it easier to deal with.

First of all, we have to remember that our job is to make an effort, but the real source of our *parnasah* is Hashem. That means that if we enjoy what we do, it doesn't take away from the command, "By the sweat of your brow shall you eat bread." You can break a sweat from lifting weights or you could instead do it by playing ball or dancing or jumping on a trampoline, but one of them is likely more enjoyable for you. That's why we should always look for work that matches our natural proclivities, and that we will enjoy, while following the other statements of *Chazal* about work that is clean, light, honorable, etc.

But there's another aspect I'd like to focus on. We can look at our jobs and see them as that necessary evil, or we can see them as a springboard for mitzvos and good. For example: recently, I updated my website JewishSpeechWriter.com and when the web designer was done, I thanked him and said "*tizku l'mitzvos.*" Why? Because he had just helped me set up a Shabbos page which would say, "Closed in Honor of Shabbat" if someone tried to view it on

Shabbos. As I often have visitors who may not be *Shomer Shabbos*, I hope this message will cause a *kiddush Hashem* and perhaps make them think a little.

Now, he could look at it that he did his "job," or he can feel that he just participated in a *kiddush Hashem*. Which one do you think would make the job lighter and more satisfying?

I spoke to a fellow who works at a restaurant which opens on *motza'ei Shabbos* for maybe an hour and a half or two hours in the summertime. He sighed, "I wonder if it's even worth it to open."

"Are you kidding?" I told him, "Look, there's a couple who finally got a chance to go out together for a little while without the kids; you've got people eating *melaveh malkah*; there are visitors from out-of-town who are able to get a bite to eat. Look at all the people whose lives you've improved and the mitzvos you enabled to be performed because you were open." He smiled, and I think he took a new look at his job.

When people ask me what I do, I say I'm a writer. (I have a day job, but I don't think it's my essence as much as my writing.) I write speeches, *divrei Torah*, and a magazine column. Sometimes I add I'm involved in *chinuch*, because that's the outlook I have on it. Now sometimes it gets difficult, like when I'm two days past deadline or when I have to get up at 4 A.M. to get the Migdal Ohr, my weekly *dvar Torah*, done in time. But that doesn't faze me so much because I'm focused on the chance to do so much good and affect so many others positively.

Whatever you do, you can find the wonderful mitzvos in it. If you're a doctor, nurse, teacher, firefighter or EMT, it's probably easy, but everyone can do it. If you're a tailor or seamstress, focus on how you help others look and feel good about themselves.

Sanitation engineer? You're enabling people to make *berachos* and breathe clean air.

Work in a call center? Smile when you're on the phone and put others in a good mood.

In business? Deal honestly and fulfill *Choshen Mishpat* as well as make a *kiddush Hashem.*

Sell insurance? Think how you're making a difficult time just a bit easier.

Stay-at-home mom? You're empowering your spouse to fulfill his mitzvos and raising generations of precious Jews to serve *HaKadosh Baruch Hu.* When you change a diaper, don't think "Ugh, what a mess," but "*Baruch Hashem*, he/she will be comfortable and happy now."

Even if you can't figure out how to connect your job to mitzvos, you can remember that just by working you are doing a mitzvah because you're fulfilling Hashem's command to be involved in a job. Whatever you do, you have the choice and the chance. Instead of looking at the difficulties, we can look at the opportunities. Then those jobs will seem a lot less like work.

A Father's Love

S EVERAL YEARS AGO, I was fortunate enough to spend *Yom Tov* at a hotel where Rabbi Yissachar Frand was the "scholar-in-residence." He spoke at the different services and gave lectures throughout the week. I saw people accosting him all day and night with questions and comments.

While I might have approached him, I felt bad bothering him when so many others already had. I noticed that his table in the dining room had a partition around it presumably to afford his family at least a modicum of privacy during their meals. It was therefore with hesitation that I approached and parted the curtains before lunch one day.

"I'm sorry to bother you; I know you're busy," I began, as he looked up from the table, "but I just wanted to tell you what a nice young man your son is. He came over to me and made conversation, and was really so outgoing. It was a pleasure speaking with him and I wanted to let you know."

He broke out into a huge grin and said, "Let me tell you something. A father is never too busy to hear something nice about his child. Thank you for telling me."

His reaction really stuck with me. Since then, I've made it a point to tell people nice things about their kids and invariably they take great pleasure in the compliments. It's unusual, I guess, because most of us just take things for granted. Taking the time to say something really makes a difference though. As they say, "If you see something, say something."

When it comes to my own children, I know I love hearing nice things about them, but of course, as we age, the stories of a job well done become rarer. Again, I think it's because of expectations. It should be a priority for all of us to say nice things about our children and other people's as well.

I also realized that when my children squabble, it upsets me. If one tattles on the other and says something mean, I tell her, "Don't talk that way about my daughter!" Even when it's from our own kids, we want to hear good things about our children.

I can attest to the fact that I let them get away with a lot more when they're playing nicely together, and that I'm quicker to be strict when they aren't getting along with each other. Sometimes I wonder if they understand that when they complain about their siblings I'm not running to their rescue because it makes me look critically at them as well. I feel like they think that if they convince me that "she made a mean face at me" or "she took my book without asking" I will suddenly cast aside any love I have for the other child and focus on the complainer's needs alone.

Maybe it's just me, but that's not how I roll. I'm quicker to be generous when my child says something nice about her sister, or when she suffers in silence. I notice what goes on, and I have my own reasons behind when and to what I choose to respond. Let's extrapolate from that.

I'm a father who loves his children, yet when they harm each other, I prefer to deal with it on my own instead of having them accuse each other. When they misbehave, but do it together, I have more patience because of the pleasure I get from seeing them interact peacefully and with love.

HaKadosh Baruch Hu is Our Father too. He has His methods of punishing bad behavior, and He doesn't miss anything. Parents are supposed to have eyes in the back of their heads; Hashem has eyes everywhere. We sometimes misbehave, and He has to deal with it.

Now that I know how I am as a father, and I know that Rabbi Frand feels the same way about hearing nice things about *his* kids, I think it's a pretty safe bet that it's the same way Hashem feels about *His* kids.

If we complain about others and are critical of them, Hashem is more likely (based solely on my own self-assessment, of course) to look critically at us. We don't need to tell Him their shortcomings because He already knows them. In fact, He probably put them there in the first place!

By putting people down, we're speaking ill of Hashem's children. As a father, I know how hearing bad about my children would upset me — why should Hashem be any different? Is it any wonder that when people don't treat each other nicely bad things happen?

If you're reading this, and thinking that I can't possibly know what Hashem's feelings are, I'd like to make one more point. I already know that other fathers are happy when they hear nice things about their kids, and now I can prove that when we don't get along and disparage Hashem's children bad things happen.

The *talmidim* of R' Akiva were so great and yet they died during the time of the *Sefirah*. Why? Because they did not treat each other with honor. In other words, they didn't speak nicely about Hashem's children! My theory is much closer to being proved, and there are *Chazal*s which will bear it out.

So the next time you have the chance to say something nice about a fellow Jew, even if there's even more to say that isn't nice, give the *Ribono shel Olam* the *nachas* of speaking nicely about His children. If we show Him we can get along, we will realize that our lives are much richer, much more peaceful, and we will be protected from all harm.

When Life Gives You Lemons

*T*HERE'S AN EXPRESSION ABOUT being upbeat and making the best of things: "When life gives you lemons, make lemonade." The idea behind that is despite going through some tough times, you can sweeten them up and find a way to turn the negative around and come out with a positive.

I thought about this one day when I was in a bookstore and saw a cookbook with a big slice of lemon on the cover. At that magnification, I took notice of the tiny pockets of juice encased in the pale, translucent flesh of this tart fruit. It got me to thinking.

We use lemons and lemon juice as a metaphor for sour or disagreeable events in our life. We figure that somehow, by adding other things, you can get past the unpleasantness, overpower the negative, and make something good out of it. But I think we're missing the point.

R' Avigdor Miller *z"l* talks about an orange. How it has a sturdy wrapper, with a bright attractive color on the outside, and it is full of sweet juice and vitamins. Hashem created it in this fashion for our benefit. We see the color and want to eat it. Want proof? The inside of the peel is white. Why? Because you don't see it.

Well, lemons are bright and pretty too. They have a sunshiny-yellow color and the same protective cover as oranges. And yet, they get a bad rap because they make you pucker. But if they were so bad, why would the Creator make them such a nice beckoning color?

The truth is that lemons are pretty amazing. Like oranges, they are full of vitamins. It's just that we human beings have a hard time swallowing the sourness of the lemon. Which is where those little pouches come in.

I believe that Hashem makes the lemons with those little separate compartments of juice so we're not overwhelmed by the tartness. A little is flavorful; a lot is painful.

If we imagine those bursts of tanginess which make our faces twist up and contort as corresponding to challenges in life, we can see that *HaKadosh Baruch Hu* ensures that we only get just enough tartness at one time so that we're not overcome by it.

Lemons get their pucker from citric acid. Know what else lemon juice is good for? Tenderizing meat. The acid breaks down the collagen of the meat and makes it more tender. Of course, leave it on too long and the meat will start to cure, becoming tough and dry.

Similarly, troubles and challenges can help us grow and develop by breaking down the barriers to our growth, the misconceptions and arrogance, and softening us with humility. If we look at the difficult situations in life, we will recognize that most of the time they come in squirts and spurts that are enough to make us think, but not to get us so hardened and cynical as to become dried out.

When we recognize that such situations are there not to hurt us but to help us change, we don't need anything else to sweeten the juice into lemonade, because we will realize the benefits of the troubles themselves and thank God for them.

Which is why I believe lemons are such a sunny color of yellow. It is a message for us to learn and recognize that this should make us happy. A person is obligated to thank Hashem for the "bad" in life with the same *simchah* that he thanks Him for the good. That's because if we get to the essence of problems and challenges, they are not bad, but good and good for us.

Imagine you went to lift weights, and you used a one-pound dumbbell. Sure, you'd be moving the weight, but your muscles wouldn't grow because you weren't placing any strain on them. To really see improvement, you need to constantly move past your comfort zone.

When life gives you lemons, that's God's way of helping you grow. He's like a personal trainer, devoted to seeing you in perfect form — emotionally, intellectually, and spiritually. If He always put you in comfortable situations, your character wouldn't get stronger. You'd just be the same lumpy mush of a man or woman as you were when you were five or six, unable to face disappointment or frustration.

So, the next time you experience something that causes you discomfort, remember the humble lemon, and how the tartness comes in small doses. You only get challenges in portions you can handle. Remember that it is a great meat tenderizer. Think about how you might change and grow from the experience. And remember that it has a bright yellow color to symbolize that yes, this really is good for you.

Then go make some lemonade, sit back, and calmly ride out the storm.

Objects in the Mirror

HAVE YOU EVER NOTICED the little phrase on the bottom of car mirrors? It says, "Objects in mirror are closer than they appear." That's because the mirrors we have on the car are intended to give us a more sweeping view so they seem to make items smaller. The warning tells us not to look at them as normal representations of distance or depth.

I think human beings are given a similar perspective when it comes to objects in their mirrors — themselves. In the case of humans, however, it seems to be reversed. It is the objects in the mirror, US, that seem bigger and more important than anything around us.

That's when we'd be wise to heed the message that we're not, in fact, seeing objectively and must make appropriate adjustments to avoid disaster.

Swallowing the "Bitter" Pill

THOSE OF US WHO are able to swallow medicines with ease may sometimes find it amusing how others who are not so blessed deal with their problem. I know that when I was younger I would laugh when I saw my mother trying to swallow pills. First, she tried with a sip of water. No dice. Then more sips and some encouraging waving, as if directing the pills down her throat telepathically.

While that worked sometimes, other times found her bargaining and threatening them. "Come on you little buggers, go down. Come on, you can do it. Let's go, now!"

As a last resort came applesauce, as if her throat wouldn't know what her brain and eyes helped her hands to do in putting the pill on the spoon and would swallow it when it's camouflaged. Looking back, I realize that it's no laughing matter. I feel bad for people who experience such difficulty, and so should we all.

Now, while many of us may not be able to relate to that difficulty in specific, I think we can relate to having a hard time swallowing other bitter things.

Recently, I was at a *simchah* when an unfortunate fellow had an verbal outbreak of what appeared to be Tourette's syndrome. He was flushed and began angrily spouting obscenities while flailing his arms wildly. As it turns out, he was not suffering from Tourette's, but was rather discussing a certain person for whom he had a dislike. I must tell you that though I tried to calm him down, it only served to make him angrier when I asked him not to use such violent and vulgar language, let alone about another Jew.

Someone else I know can tell you how he was wronged by a certain individual (and it's not so clear that he was wronged at all) going back half a dozen years. When he retells the story, you can see him getting visibly agitated.

I feel the same pity for these people as I do for the person hopelessly waving the pill towards his or her stomach. Unfortunately, they were faced with a bitter pill they simply cannot swallow. The worst part of it is that because they can't swallow it, they remain sick and get even sicker about things.

Instead of taking life's bumps and bruises as lessons, or as God's little instant messages, they take them personally and can't imagine that they ever deserve to be treated that way. David HaMelech's response to be cursed was, "*Nu*, Hashem told him to curse David, why should I be upset if he was following the word of Hashem?"

Now, before you say, "But what this guy did to me wasn't Hashem's will, he did it because he's a lousy sniveling weasel," remember that nearly all *Rishonim* agree that nobody can help or harm you if it is not decreed in *Shamayim*.

Then remember something you say every day in *davening*, three times a day, "May my soul be as dust to everyone." You got what you asked for, someone treated you like dirt! So what's the problem? The problem is we don't see ourselves the same way.

If we saw ourselves as frail creatures with shortcomings of our own, we might not be so quick to judge someone for mistreating us. First of all, we wouldn't let it bother us because we recognize that it's coming from Hashem for a purpose, even if we don't know what that purpose is.

Secondly, we'd realize that other people, too, are struggling with being the best human beings they can, and it's not an easy job. Other people can be petty and thoughtless and their affronts on our personal honor don't mean all that much. We're better off ignoring the messenger and focusing on why this had to happen to us (which it did).

Finally, as the Gemara says, people who are too *makpid* get bellyaches. Why not save yourself the aggravation and get over the insult? When you bear a grudge, you're still the one bearing it while the other party may have long forgotten it. You make yourself sick waiting for what? An apology? Divine retribution?

Don't waste your time. Just accept that things happen and move on with your life. And if that seems hard to swallow, try some applesauce.

In the Market for Growth

*C*HAZAL TELL US THAT when *Klal Yisrael* is doing the will of Hashem, their work will be done by others. I don't know whether I'm doing the will of Hashem, but my job was definitely made easier by whoever makes up all these special holidays.

According to the United States Census Bureau and Chase's Calendar of Events, which its publisher McGraw-Hill says is, "the most comprehensive and authoritative reference available on special events, worldwide holidays and festivals, civic observances, historic anniversaries, famous birthdays and much more," February is Return Shopping Carts to the Supermarket Month.

Can you believe it? A whole month dedicated to one of the most common problems in our society. Some in the Jewish community like to call it the "Cart Crisis," but it's been going on for so long that hardly anybody even thinks about it anymore.

Cart Month was the idea of Anthony Dinolfo, a grocery store owner whose carts had turned up just about everywhere imaginable. As he watched the 1969 historic event of Neil Armstrong walking on the moon, he had amusing thought. "I said I wouldn't be surprised if he found a shopping cart in one of the craters," Dinolfo told the Chicago Sun-Times.

Now, most of the places you hear about this festival will talk about the financial losses to the stores (each cart can run $100 or more) or the impact on the environment (for example at treehugger.com — and no, I'm not making up that name).

There are even special guidelines about how to celebrate "Return Your Carts to the Supermarket Month." Here's what I've found:

- Return your cart to a designated "cart rack" or aisle. These can be found in various places throughout the parking lot or near the store's entrance.
- Leave your cart near the entrance and carry grocery bags to your vehicle by hand. It'll be courteous to another customer.
- Take a cart that is near your vehicle to shop with instead of taking one by the entrance. This method helps out the courtesy clerks and prevents the homeless from capturing a cart.
- Ask the cashier or bagger to double the bags. If you have to walk somewhere, don't use a cart to assist you in carrying things.
- Have a bagger escort the cart to the vehicle to help you unload groceries. He or she then will wheel the cart back to a designated area.
- If you are shopping light, take a basket instead.

Many places now currently have devices installed on the wheels, so that the carts lock up when going past a marked line. What I see from here is that they're more worried about runaway carts disappearing from the stores than what I am concerned about. You see, I find the problem to be that the carts very much stay in the parking lot, just strewn across it and blocking parking spaces from being used by the next customer.

Of course, we have good excuses, because we are in a hurry, but how many times have you come home to find that had you been there fifteen seconds earlier (the approximate time it takes to put the cart in the right place) you would have won a million dollars? Okay, what if it was fifteen minutes? Probably not such a biggie either.

Often, we figure that we're in a hurry so every second counts. If we stopped and thought about it, we'd realize that the extra few seconds won't make much difference to us, but will to someone else.

For example, you're leaving the grocery store where you spent a leisurely hour shopping, shmoozing, and calling your house to find out what else you were supposed to pick up. Now, you come outside, unpack your groceries into your car, stop to talk to a friend who hasn't yet gone in, and suddenly don't have the extra few moments it takes to bring the cart to the store. No problem! Leave it in the handicapped parking space. That person with the wheelchair-accessible van won't mind parking on the other side of the lot. "If they knew how many things I had to do, they'd understand."

Now that person comes and can't park there. As it just snowed, there are very few spots that can accommodate their van so they end up driving around for five minutes (blessing you every inch of the way), and all because you couldn't be bothered.

Okay, so you're more courteous and leave the handicapped space alone. Instead, you carefully angle the cart at the front corner of your spot. That smart move saves you a precious 1.56 seconds, except that you have to go back and readjust it when it starts to roll. Otherwise, it would have been a smart move.

Now, your sister-in-law comes to shop and, seeing a spot open from afar, zooms in, only to screech to a halt halfway in when she sees the cart previously obscured from vision. Real nice.

The most cosmically-satisfying scenario I saw was when someone couldn't be bothered to bring her cart to the store so she lamely shoved it towards the front door and drove off. That's fine except that when she backed up, she let out a loud expletive as she slammed into a cart some idiot had left halfway between the parking spots and the door. Oh yeah… that was her.

I was in Florida recently and I was about to pull into a spot when I saw there was a cart in it. I moved down a few spaces, then on my way to the store, went and got the cart from the space. A woman who saw me asked if I needed it and I said, "I was just moving it so somebody could park there." She was amazed. "That's so nice!"

As I had a yarmulke, which probably stands out quite a bit in South Florida, I know I made a *kiddush Hashem*. Had I been in Monsey, where most of the people at the supermarkets I go to are Jewish, I could have gotten even more mitzvos for thinking about others and fulfilling *V'ahavtah l'rei'acha kamocha*.

So when you go shopping in the month of February, grab a cart from the lot and bring it in to the store with you. Leave your cart at the front instead of making people run a slalom course in the lot, and actively think of the people you're helping and how you're improving your own *middos*.

Take the extra few seconds to turn indifference into a cause for celebration.

Carrying a Tune

THE STORY IS TOLD about R' Boruch Ber Leibowitz *z"l* that some- one once approached him and asked how it was that he had such a beautiful singing voice, while his *rebbi*, R' Chaim Brisker *z"l* was a less than capable singer.

R' Boruch Ber was dumbfounded as he wrestled with the mere suggestion that his beloved master could be less than perfect. He stood there a few moments, until his brow cleared and he smiled. "The *Ribono shel Olam* would not wish to make a person have every *ma'alah* (good attribute)," he said, "or they would not be hu- man. My *rebbi* was perfect in every other way so *HaKadosh Baruch Hu* made sure he didn't have the best voice. I, on the other hand, have no other redeeming qualities, so, out of mercy, He at least gave me a nice voice."

In my case, I can't even get to R' Boruch Ber's feeling of imper- fection because even my voice is far less than spectacular. While most often I am considered a capable *baal tefillah*, able to follow *nusach* relatively well, with a voice that doesn't totally grate on people's ears, I would not consider my voice sweet.

On top of that, I have another problem. Carrying a tune.

Over the years I have witnessed many wonderful *baalei tefillah* who weave beautiful *niggunim* throughout their *davening*; whose *Kedushos* draw in the whole *tzibbur* to an inspiring chorus of joy- ful, awe-inducing harmony, and who always have a different tune each time they *daven*.

Not me.

As Ulysses S. Grant said about his own lack of musical ability, "I only know two songs — One is Hail to the Chief, and the other one isn't." My repertoire of musical adaptations for *davening* is limited to a small handful of well-used tunes, learned over many years of listening.

In fact, my musical growth was further stunted when I *davened Kabbalas Shabbos* in tenth grade. I was singing *Lecha Dodi* when I forgot the tune. I couldn't remember how it went and nobody helped me start the next stanza. It was the longest minute and a half of my life, and it only lasted about two seconds. What seemed like an eternity to me was really not long enough for anyone to jump in and help me, while I felt the deafening silence washing over me like a tidal wave. Panicking, I started the tune from the beginning and continued. I was so embarrassed that I never *davened* for the *amud* there again.

It would only be years later, after I had left yeshivah, that I realized I had not messed up the tune, but in fact sung it correctly. That version of *Lecha Dodi* did begin again where I had done so. Nevertheless, I was scarred for life.

Even today, when I *daven Shacharis*, I only have two tunes for *Kedushah*. One is a tune I learned in yeshivah which was sung by a *kollel* fellow I looked up to. It was a very popular song at the time, so I actually knew the words and tune, plus the message of the *tefillah* recorded in that melody resonates very strongly with me. From listening to him, I knew how it fit into the words of *Kedushah*. Today, when I sing it, I can often get some of the *tzibbur* to sing with me as they also recall the song from their youth.

But then there's another song I remember. Often, it pops into my head and I will sing it purely because I enjoy it. I think it's beautiful even if not that many people know it. It's a tune that was used for *Eishes Chayil* on an album a decade or so ago, which was marginally successful (okay, maybe it went double-platinum, I don't really know music so I can't tell).

I didn't know the tune from the album, but rather because the composer went to yeshivah with me, and frequently used the tune for *Shacharis*; and now I do too.

I got to thinking one day. Why is it that of all the songs I've heard in my life it's that one I remember? It could be because he sang that tune for *Eishes Chayil* every week, or because I just found the melody to be pleasant, nearly every one of the hundred and sixty-two *thousand* times I heard him sing it. But I don't think so. I think there's another reason it means so much to me.

You see, when he used to sing it in yeshivah, before it went public, sometimes the *bachurim* who knew the tune decided to play a joke on him and would not sing with him. He would launch into his melodious warbling with gusto, but it was instantly recognizable that his was the solitary voice in the large *beis midrash*.

But then, one voice would join him. One voice, which felt terrible that people could be so cruel, would do its best to keep up with the rising and falling of the notes and the tenor and pitch of the melody. One voice joined another in solidarity and compassion. My voice. I couldn't bear to see him embarrassed so I would sing my best, trying to camouflage the fact that others weren't singing with him.

When I sing this song today, I feel proud. Proud that I overcame the urge to conform and be like everyone else, even if it meant risking popularity; proud that I was sensitive to someone's feelings; proud that I opened my mouth with wisdom. I guess that's why I can carry this tune above all others, because in truth, this is a tune which carries me.

Shaliach Mitzvah Money

R ECENTLY I NEEDED TO go on a trip. When I told my *chavrusa* that I'd be away, he said to me, "Oh, here's some *shaliach mitzvah* money." I took the dollar from him and put it into my wallet, folded in a strange way, so I would remember what it was for. When I went to shul in Buffalo, I pulled out that dollar and put it in the *tzedakah* box. As I did so, I smiled. I'm not sure why, perhaps it was like getting a freebie. Y'know, I got to give *tzedakah*, but it didn't come out of my pocket directly? Of course, that also means I don't get the mitzvah, but sometimes our minds play tricks on us.

Well, the next week, my other *chavrusa* told me *he* was going away. I reached into my pocket and pulled out a dollar for him to give. He thanked me and put it in his wallet. I got to thinking about it.

We give people "*shaliach mitzvah*" money because of the *Chazal* that says "*Shaluchei mitzvah einan nizakin* — Emissaries involved in a mitzvah do not come to harm," hence the name "*shaliach mitzvah* money." The point is that somehow, by giving them our dollar, they will be protected from all harm.

That may be the case, but what if someone already has money from someone else, or they were going for a *dvar mitzvah* anyway? Are they more "protected?" Is it like wearing suspenders and a belt? Should they say thank you if they're not getting any added protection?

I was thinking about it and realized that when a friend gives you *shaliach mitzvah* money, he's saying "I like you enough that I hope you live through the trip." He cares about you and wants you to survive whether you're taking a simple trip upstate, or a more dangerous trip to Israel, Iraq, or to see your mother-in-law.

It's an investment in you that says "You're worth a dollar to me, and I want to see you again." How often have people made us feel like two cents? Now, here's some guy or girl who makes us feel like we're worth fifty times that. While this isn't a huge amount, it's still nice to know that someone cares.

Well, this line of thought got me to think about the next stage. Do you have to wait until someone leaves to let them know you care? The old adage says, "absence makes the heart grow fonder." A friend of mine used to tell his wife, "Go away, I want to miss you."

But those cases aside, why not take the time to tell people that you are happy to have them around? If you see your friend, child, spouse, and start to smile, why not tell them you're glad they're alive? Of course, at that point they'll probably smell your breath to see if you've been taste-testing the Shabbos shnapps again or dipping into the cooking sherry, but who cares? You'll make them feel good about themselves and brighten their day.

One way of understanding how *shaliach mitzvah* money works is as follows: You see, we have a concept of *levayah*, accompanying someone when they leave on a trip. Doing so historically alerted any bandits watching people leaving the city that there was someone who cared about them and the bandits would back off for fear of retribution. One could say that we do the same when a person dies, so that the prosecuting angels know the deceased has a crack defense team on their side. [Note: Don't quote me on this. I'm under a deadline to write this so I'm making it up as I go along.]

That being said, when you give money to someone going on a trip, you alert those same angels not to mess with your buddy, or they'll have to answer to you. They tend to back off when people care for one another like that.

In addition, when you cheer up someone, you can change their outlook, and in turn, their *mazel*. Having a different *mazel* may protect him from anything bad befalling him. Or at least, it can make him feel better about it if anything does happen.

So, the next time you see someone you care about, or at least someone you'd be disappointed if you heard he'd fallen off the face of the planet, let him know that he's worth a buck to you, or at least a quarter. Trust me, you'll get back more than you gave, and most likely a nice chunk of change.

That's What Money Is For

ONE FRIDAY, MY WIFE called me. She had purchased a dress that she wanted to wear for Shabbos, but when she went to the store she couldn't find the coupon she thought she had, and the only way to get the credit from the store later was to keep the tags on and bring it back with the coupon. What should she do?

"Do you want to wear the dress for *this* Shabbos?" I asked. "Yes," she replied.

"Then the extra money is for *kavod Shabbos*. It's worth it." (Maybe I spoke too soon; I didn't know how much the dress cost…)

An hour later, she called to tell me she had found a better coupon than she was expecting and she was on the way to the store to get the credit. She got the money back and got to wear it for Shabbos. And I got the *zechus* of honoring both my wife and Shabbos, and it didn't cost me a penny!

I could have told her to wait and wear something else, and planned to save the money, but what am I saving it for? *Chazal* tell us that righteous people value their money more than their own bodies. This is often misconstrued that money has importance of its own. Far from it. *Tzaddikim* love money because of what they can do with it.

Here, I had an opportunity to honor Shabbos, a special day for cultivating our relationship with Hashem, and it would only cost me a few dollars. On top of that, I had a chance to spend money on my wife, who takes care of me and my children; enables me to learn Torah, often sending me out to a *shiur* even when I'm exhausted; who encourages me and is proud of how I try to help people and inspire them with my writing and speaking; and who is herself such a good and caring friend to so many. I had a chance to do something for a person like that, do you think I'd let such an opportunity slip away from me?

It's funny. People often hesitate to spend money on their wives and on Shabbos, yet *Chazal* have told us that these things are *segulos* for becoming wealthy. They think that by being stingy they will have more money, but in reality they are choking off the sources of *berachah* in their life.

Of course, being stingy is nothing new. The very first person to be stingy was recorded in the Torah. His name was Kayin. Heard of him? He brought a *korban* to Hashem which was a great idea. The problem was that he was cheap about it so Hashem ignored it. Hashem told him that if he ever wanted to succeed he had to spend money when it came to spiritual things. Hevel, of course, did that right off the bat, when he brought from the best of his flocks and Hashem sent him an immediate sign of acceptance and approval.

But what are considered spiritual uses of money? Of course you understand that buying good food for Shabbos is one, and giving *tzedakah* to a poor person is too. But what about energizing your "mundane" expenditures with a boost of *ruchnius*?

A friend who cleans carpets told me a harrowing story. A very *frum* woman called him to her home for an estimate. He quoted her a reasonable price and she began to haggle. "Last year, a non-Jewish carpet cleaner quoted me ten dollars cheaper. Either you go down in your price or I'm going to call the *goy*." That was it. Her money was more valuable to her than patronizing a Jew. Was she right?

Rashi in *Parshas Behar* quotes a *Toras Kohanim* that states that one should patronize a Jew when possible. Although this is not recorded as law in the Rambam and *Shulchan Aruch*, the Chafetz

Chayim in *Ahavas Chesed* and *Nesiv HaChesed* rules that one should follow this policy. Even if the Jewish-owned business is located a bit further away and it will take longer to shop there, or it costs a little more, it is still a mitzvah to give preference to the Jewish-owned establishment. *Poskim* discuss how much more one should spend to do business with a Jew. Most say somewhere between a fifth and a sixth (15%–20%) more is appropriate. The Chafetz Chaim says this is one of the highest forms of *tzedakah*, using our money for the right purposes.

While I was thinking about this article, I saw a great story in R' Leibie Sternberg's weekly *dvar Torah*. The first Belzer Rebbe, the "Sar Shalom" was orphaned at an early age. His father used to patronize a gentile shoemaker and would always haggle and try to knock down the price. When a Jewish shoemaker opened up, he was so happy because now he took his shoes exclusively there and often gave extra money to the shoemaker.

His father explained. "As long as I dealt with the non-Jew, I was afraid of the prohibition of giving a gift to a gentile. Now I am so thrilled to be able to patronize a *Yid* that I want to give even more money."

My friend told me another story. He bid for a job at a school. It was a huge job, involving lots of shlepping and hard work. His bid came in at $50 more than the Polish cleaner who had just left. "Why are you so much more?" he was asked.

"Why are my prices higher?" he asked incredulously. "When I shop, I go to a Kosher supermarket, he goes to Shoprite or Pathmark. It costs me twice as much. I pay tuition for *yeshivos*, and he sends his kids to public school for free. I have expenses for *Yom Tov* that he never heard of. And besides," he concluded, "when you need money to pay your teachers, who are you going to call for a donation — him or me?"

"W-Well, you have to understand," stammered the school representative, "this is *mammon hekdesh*."

Guess what, folks? So is this. When you spend your money at the Jewish stores, or hire Jewish workers even if it costs you a little more, you are turning your money into *mammon hekdesh*, "Hashem's money." You are following the spiritual initiatives of Hevel in understanding what Hashem wants us to do with our money.

And, as my friend pointed out, it's cyclical. When you give your money to a Jew, it's going back into your community and generating mitzvos as he pays for tuition, food, Shabbos items and so on. When you hire the cheapest person no matter who they are, your money could be used for the worst of things. Would that really be worth the ten bucks?

He also told me that Pesach has become a huge competition in his industry as people from all around flock to offer cleaning services because they know that for Pesach the Jews clean their carpets. He knows that a few of his competitors are Jewish, but many more are not. And he knows that people will look to save a buck.

Well, let me share something with all of you. Did you know that when you sell your *chametz* before Pesach the Rav often does several different *kinyanim*? There are major differences of opinion in *halachah* about how to transact business with gentiles so they try to cover as many bases as possible. What's the big deal? Why not just look in the Gemara and see what they did?

The reason is because there's no Gemara that talks about doing business with gentiles. In those times it was unheard of. While today things have changed, and we constantly do business with non-Jews, we should never forget that our first choice should be to invest in our own communities and our own people. What goes around really does come around.

So, as you're spending $16 for a package of *Pesachdik* cookies, or paying the higher prices while shopping at the Jewish stores, make sure you don't follow the stinginess of Cain. Just remind yourself that you are turning your money into *ruchnius*, and do it as long as you are "Abel."

Life Is a Highway
(Or At Least a Highly-Congested Urban Intersection)

D RIVING IS A PART of American life and our attachment to cars, buses and other mechanical conveyances is pervasive. It's even entered our vocabulary. "You're driving me crazy!" "He's driving me up a wall!" "You're gonna drive me to drink!" You see? We use driving in our speech all the time. The funny thing is that it all has a similar connotation of frustration and exasperation.

Why should that be? When compared to horses, cars are much easier to deal with. You don't have to worry about your car getting spooked by another car, you don't have to feed it constantly, and your car never wakes you up at night with loud whinnying and braying noises that alarm you... ummmm.... ok... well... at least you don't have to worry about it getting spooked.

So what is it about cars that drives us bananas? I'd have to say that it honestly isn't the cars, but rather the people behind the wheel. And I don't mean specifically the people themselves, just who they become when they're behind the wheel.

Driving gives people a sense of power, a sense of privilege, a sense of humor. I mean, why else would someone block traffic to converse with their friend if they didn't think it was a big joke to hear people honking in annoyance? They laugh and ignore it, often waving drivers around (as if they could fit) with a dismissive and condescending gesture.

I guess it might be because when we're insulated in our own little worlds, we don't view the outdoors as real. Everything beyond the windshield is just a display, like in a storefront window, there for our amusement.

Let me give you an example. When an ambulance or police car comes from behind you, the law is that you are supposed to move to the right and stop, regardless of the direction they're coming from. That way, the emergency vehicle can drive down the center of the road if need be. How many times have we seen people speed up when they hear sirens but keep driving? Of course, nobody reading this has ever done it. But the truth is, we sometimes get confused.

I once had to make a left turn and was in the turning lane when a cop with lights flashing and sirens blaring barreled down the opposite center lane right at me. I froze. I couldn't move to the right because I had to make a turn. To his shock, I just sat there. Finally, he frantically waved his hand to show that I should move. It woke me from my reverie and I shifted over.

You'll be happy to know that I eventually made my way back to the turning lane and my destination so I know that moving over is not permanently damaging. I'm not an indifferent person, but I reacted wrongly in that case.

A woman I know witnessed the following scene and almost called me at 11 P.M. one night to tell me about it so it could end up in an article. She was on a two-lane road (one in each direction, no shoulders at all) and there was an accident ahead. It looked bad and she could see several Hatzolah ambulances coming up from behind. She dutifully pulled to the right as the ambulances whooshed past her and helped the victims, quickly ensuring that everyone was okay while concerned drivers looked on quietly from their parked cars. Well, that would be a nice story, but that's not what happened.

She did move over, but the cars ahead of her were more concerned about whether they would get home five minutes later than whether the people in the accident would ever get home.

With lights flashing in their rearview mirrors, at least three cars in front of her made a slow, deliberate K-turn (supposedly a three-point turn) to get themselves out of the jam so they could go a different way. (What kind of turn is it when it takes sixteen times of moving forward and back to turn around? I dunno, maybe that's a Special K turn.) Because of this, it took the ambulances about six extra minutes to get to the victims. These drivers didn't think about the victims or their families, or how they would feel if they were lying in a pool of blood and a pile of shattered glass. (Don't worry, though, the fifty or sixty people who walked over from their homes and apartments and crowded around to watch the show eventually moved aside for the emergency crews.)

Why does this happen? Because cars make us feel important and powerful. They have a way of making us forget that others exist. Maybe that's why driving goes together with insanity. Being alone in your own little world makes you start to talk to yourself and lose touch with reality.

Life is a highway. Things fly by, but the intelligent and observant driver will pay attention to his surroundings and make sure he's heading in the right direction. (Note: This paragraph is a metaphor. If you're reading and interpreting it in its simplest form, make a U-turn and try again.)

A car can be a great source of pride. If it's an expensive car and others can't afford it, that's one kind of pride, the kind that doesn't come with any joy.

If, on the other hand, your car is meant to get you where you need to go, or to help others, not make you into someone you're not, you just might get somewhere. There's a pride that comes from understanding that everything in this world has its place and purpose and by not giving in to the temptation of focusing on yourself and "putting yourself in the driver's seat," you're showing that you are a courteous driver.

Now, if you don't drive, or don't have a car, imagine the other times and ways you tune out other people and see if you can find some opportunities to get yourself in gear and focus on the world around you. When you start to notice others, I bet you'll find yourself getting a lift. If nothing else, when you do so you will truly have arrived.

Objects in Mirror Are Closer Than They Appear

*H*AVE YOU EVER LOOKED at one of those reversible bathroom/ make-up mirrors? When you look at it close up, your face is brought into intense scrutiny and you can see every line, wrinkle, freckle and bump. But what happens when you flip it over?

YOUR FACE IS NOW GIANT AND DISTORTED AND YOUR PORES LOOK LIKE CRATERS ON THE LUNAR SURFACE.

I find those mirrors disconcerting and try to avoid them. I don't think anyone should have to view their nostrils that close up.

In life, I think we run into people or experience situations intended to make us take a look at ourselves and see our own actions as they appear from the outside. Rabbi Twerski has a chapter in one of his books entitled, "The World as a Mirror." I like that. That's what this article is about.

On Rosh Hashanah, one of the *kabalos* I accepted upon myself was to be more careful with speaking idle talk in shul. Now, this isn't just a nice thing, it's a real halachic issue. I must admit I often find myself falling into the trap of socializing or speaking non-*davening* related things in shul or *beis midrash*, but at least I'm trying to quit.

Recently, I had an opportunity to figuratively look in the mirror. Unfortunately (or fortunately) it was one of those multi-magnifying mirrors which grotesquely disfigure everything.

I was in shul after *davening* trying to review the *parshah*. Now, *Onkelos* is hard enough without distractions, but this made it nearly impossible. Several men were loudly discussing varied and sundry topics. Who was playing in the "big game," and why they should have won, what someone had done when his grandchildren came to visit, where he bought that hat, and other such critical information.

Not only was this drivel pointless, it was loud. I couldn't think. Well, I actually could think, but I was thinking how I wished they would shut their mouths or get out of shul. I tried focusing harder, telling myself that this was Hashem's way of getting me to focus on my learning. Then it hit me. I saw my own shul-talking before my eyes, magnified and grotesquely unsettling. This must be what I sound like to others. If not to others, at least to the *Shechinah*. By using these fellows as a mirror for my own imperfections, I was able to see what I needed to fix.

Here's another one. While at a pizza shop with my family, I saw a woman at the next table with a six-month-old baby, a four-year-old girl, and two grandmothers. The little girl knocked over her cup of juice and it spilled all over, including splashing onto the baby. Her mother was incensed.

While the mother ran to get napkins, the girl apologized, and told her grandmother it was an accident, which the grandmother related to the mother upon her return. "It wasn't an accident," the mother growled through clenched teeth. "She was careless!" (which, by definition, means it was an accident, but I digress). She continued her rampage as I cringed and tried to look as if I didn't hear what was happening.

"Look! All over the baby! How could you be so stupid?!" She leaned very close to her daughter's face, glared at her and said, "YOU ARE NOT A SMART GIRL! THIS WAS SO STUPID AND CARELESS!"

Now, I don't know how many therapy sessions that's gonna take to erase, but this woman had definitely lost it. The baby didn't seem to mind the few drops of moisture, and I doubt he will re-member it later on in life. I don't think the girl will remember that she was careless, but she will definitely remember that her mother thinks she's stupid, and cares more about the baby than she does about her.

Herc's that magnifying mirror again! How many times have we said things in frustration that can have devastating effects? I'm sure this woman loves her child and doesn't plan to lock her in the car for the rest of the week like she promised to do, but in her anger she was shortsighted and couldn't hear how ridiculous she sounded.

But I did. And I took a good hard look at myself in that mirror and saw my own blemishes. Trust me, I didn't get any laugh lines from it.

So, my message here is to be aware and observe the world around you. God is showing you a mirror, but if you shut your eyes, you won't see it. Use it for the same purpose anyone uses a mirror — to see what you really look like and make changes to beautify yourself.

One Good Turn

R AISINS HAVE SAVED MY life many times. Okay, maybe not raisins, but one particular raisin named Yossi. Yes, many years ago, when the California Raisin Board decided that raisins were rather dull and boring, considered by many to be nothing more than worried grapes, they came up with an ad campaign featuring singing and dancing raisins. These became such a phenomenon that they appeared everywhere, including lunchboxes, T-shirts, and even costumes. So, here I was on Purim afternoon, running to the store for something, driven by a young man in a raisin suit, complete with white stockings and shoes.

As we approached a traffic light, the person in the car ahead of us inexplicably stopped short, and Yossi hit the brakes. At the last minute, he swerved to the right, towards the shoulder of the road, and then back left to the roadway. That extra distance, he explained, slowed us sufficiently to avoid ending up in the back seat of the car ahead of us.

Since that time, I have kept this knowledge with me and put it to good use. It has saved me from numerous accidents and much aggravation. If there is to be a spiritual counterpart to this physical means of protecting yourself from impact, I think it would be to realize that when life throws you curves, or puts obstacles in your path, you can swerve and not crash.

That was one lesson that stayed with me. Another time, when I was in yeshivah in Cleveland, a fellow named R' Getzel Fried told me a *vort* which has stayed with me. When the brothers came to Egypt, Yosef gave them changes of clothing. He gave Binyamin five changes of clothing. "*CHaMeSH*," said R' Getzel, stands for *Rosh CHodesh, [Chol ha]Mo'ed*, and **SH**abbos — three times you're supposed to change and wear nicer clothing. It must have been eighteen years ago, but I still try to dress up a little on *Rosh Chodesh* and *Chol HaMo'ed*, even when others don't. The point was that it stayed with me.

We never know what it will be that will stay with people. It could be good, or unfortunately it could be not so good. Hopefully we will do something that will have a positive impact on their lives, and they won't remember the time we had a meltdown for some reason or another.

When I was a staffer in a camp, R' Avi Shulman spoke to us and taught me another lesson which has stayed with me (and I'm pretty sure I mentioned this in the past). It's something that parents, counselors, and anyone should keep in mind.

"When you're with a camper in the summer," he told us, "in those few weeks you can teach him more than his *rebbi* can in a whole year. He will see how you act on the ball field, when you lose a game, or when you win, and it will make an impression." I try to live my life with this in mind, and I've often seen just how crucial this understanding has been.

The best part is, now that you've read this article and have an idea of how important even the smallest, most insignificant-seeming acts and even reflexes can be, you can steer clear of those bumps in the road which might make you crash or lead to untold suffering.

One good turn deserves another. Pass it on.

What Were You Thinking?

*T*HIS IS A LETTER about some specific behavior. When you read it, I hope you won't be embarrassed at being singled out, but please understand that my curiosity is overwhelming. I mean, when these things happened, I was wondering to myself: What are they thinking? So now, I'm asking YOU — What were you thinking?

When I was in line behind you at the grocery store, and you were about to have your huge cartload of items rung up while I was standing there with one item and the cash in my hand — you didn't tell me I should go ahead, you just started having your items rung up. What were you thinking? *That because you were there first you had the RIGHT to have your items rung up and make me wait?* It's true; in America you have that right. Of course, as a Jew, you're held to a higher standard.

It should have bothered you to see me standing there, knowing that you could have given me five extra minutes of my life and made a *kiddush Hashem* by courteously saying, "Oh, you have only one (or three or five) items, my check-out will take some time, please go first." I would likely have thanked you and praised you for being so thoughtful, and you would have felt so good about yourself. But that didn't happen because you didn't ask me to go first. What were you thinking?

And when your cart was finally empty, after chatting with the people on the next line, looking out the window and making silly jokes and small talk with the cashier, once you had been told the total, only then did you start to fish around for your checkbook and start writing out your check, instead of having it ready with everything but the amount filled in. So please, I must know, what were you thinking?

While I wait for that answer, I have to ask YOU something. You made the effort to be in shul. You had your *tallis* on, you had a *chumash* in front of you and you were busy talking to the guy behind you. It was *krias haTorah*, and you were almost as loud as the *baal korei*. You went through all the trouble to be in shul and then you miss the most important part of showing up — participation! Not only that, but you were disturbing others. Instead of getting the benefits of *davening* with the *minyan*, you earned yourself demerits in *Shamayim*. I have to ask — What were you thinking?

Okay, now YOU are a different story. You don't waste people's time in the store, and you don't *kibbitz* in shul. You were walking along the street one day and had to cross it. I slowed down to let you go, and waved to you to cross in front of me. You looked up and saw me, then began your trek across the road. You didn't hurry; you took your time, as if I wasn't there. Okay, I thought, maybe you had a broken leg and couldn't walk more quickly. But then I saw you run to catch the bus and you moved just fine when you wanted to. On top of that, when you crossed, you didn't wave or acknowledge the fact that I had given up my time for yours; that I had done you a favor. You showed NO gratitude. So please explain — What were you thinking?

I wish I was done, but I'm not. You asked me for help with a project. You offered to pay me for some work. I did the work, and then you said, "I'm sorry, I didn't think it would cost so much," or "Business is bad, I just don't have the money." You stalled; you made me chase you for the money. You didn't keep your word. What were you thinking?

You know that Hashem's name is *Emes*. Yaakov Avinu became

rich because he was honest even when Lavan was trying to rob him blind. You want to become rich so you violate Hashem's name because you think it will get you ahead in business? Don't you realize where *hatzlachah* comes from? Come on, what were you thinking?

Now please, don't sit back smugly thinking, "Boy, he sure told THEM!" YOU are not off the hook either. What about the time someone did something that upset you and you went off on him in public? You embarrassed him and you wouldn't back off and let him save face. You know he didn't mean to do it, that it was an accident or at least unintended, but you insisted on getting your pound of flesh. Don't you know that embarrassing someone is like killing him, only the latter is less painful? What happened to your ability to control your anger? You lashed out like a *meshuganeh* and embarrassed yourself in the process. I mean really, what were YOU thinking?

Oy, look at the time! This article is due and here I am staring in a mirror and talking to myself. What am I going to say to my readers? Maybe I'll just print this and hopefully they'll recognize some similar trait in themselves and try to change. But first, let me answer the question.

What was I thinking? It's simple — I wasn't. If I was thinking, I would never have done all those horrible things. I would have begged forgiveness right away if I had done them, but my excuse is simply that I wasn't thinking.

So now, my dear readers. Help me answer one final question: Why not?

What Ever Happened to Dinner Music?

W HEN I WAS YOUNGER, there was something I remember as the highlight of many weddings. It wasn't the *chuppah*; it wasn't the first dance; it wasn't even the smorgasbord. It was the magical time after the bandleader announced, "Ladies and Gentlemen, please find your seats, the first course is now being served."

The crowd would make their way to their tables and begin to eat their soup or whatever was being served. The band would play soft music — a faint lilting — and then it would start.

A lone figure would slowly walk to the center of the dance floor. As the music played on softly, he would begin to dance. A slow, graceful progression of twirls, circles, and steps seemed to flow silently like a blossoming flower. His limbs moved with fluidity and the beauty of it made you want to watch in silent awe. Zev, Chieli and Shmuel were some of the fellows I envied as I watched their ballet-like performance. The crowd would be spellbound, the *chasan* and *kallah* at their seats would gaze on approvingly with growing satisfaction, knowing that this act of beauty was being performed in their honor.

For their part, the dancers found no embarrassment in being the only ones on the dance floor because they were confident that their enchanting routine would give pleasure to the onlookers, especially the happy couple. They danced as if they were the only ones on earth, performing some ritual of movement, their own type of *Shirah* to the *Ribono shel Olam.*

But nowadays there is no dinner-music dancing because there is no dinner music. Instead of some quiet time to reflect on the magnitude and solemnity of the occasion, YOU ONLY HEAR THE CONSTANT "BOOM-BOOM-BOOM" OF THE BASS AND THE BLARING OF THE HORNS WHILE THE CACOPHONOUS KEYBOARD AND STRINGS ADD TO THE CHAOS —

I miss dinner music.

While the faint sounds of it wafted across the ballroom you would visit with friends, meet new people you had been seated with, and regroup before going out to the next dance and dancing your heart out. It was a moment of peace and solitude which was uplifting to the soul.

You didn't have to be moving a mile a minute; you didn't have to yell at the top of your lungs for someone to please pass the pickles. You just existed — reveling in the magical moment when the joy of the wedding got a chance to sink in. Even the band members got a chance to eat while one of their number carried the show.

So what happened?

Well, for one thing, I think people decided they wanted their money's worth from the band. "If I'm paying them I want to hear loud music from beginning to end. No time for stopping!" Now, since there are plenty of *frum*, Jewish musicians, this might somehow be a problem of "*Lo sachsom shor b'disho* — do not muzzle an ox while he's threshing." Come on, let the guys have a break, they're working hard!

It could also be that we have become so needy for constant entertainment that as an audience, if it's not rocking and banging the whole time, we're bored and disappointed. As hosts, we feel we need to entertain our guests every second of the hours-long affair. Now, you may say I'm old, and that I don't like the noise, but I can tell you that I enjoyed those times when the music was soft and the lone dancer covered the floor with marionette-like steps and bows, swaying, gliding, and turning his wrists like leaves in a gentle breeze — and I was a young man then.

Perhaps we don't want to reflect. We don't want to think or turn inside ourselves. We need the constant noise to distract us. Perhaps we are embarrassed to find beauty in something quiet, something above our base physicality. And that's a shame.

Meditation and introspection are part and parcel of being a Jew. Speaking to others and strengthening relationships are key to *Yiddishkeit*. Please, if you're reading this, don't let the music die.

If you are a musician or a *baal simchah*, do yourself and your guests a favor. Lower the volume, give people a chance to think and enjoy themselves. Let them get caught up in the beauty and emotion of the event, not in the throes of a migraine.

If you are not a musician or *baal simchah*, but often find yourself caught up in the loud and chaotic whirlwind of life, try to find a quiet oasis where you can hear yourself think. Take a break from the constant running and chasing of "things." It's more important than constantly being entertained. It's part of the beauty of life.

Let's bring back dinner music, whether at *simchah*s or just in our normal day. Turn off the noise, lose the distractions, and take the time to look around, in awe, at the wonderful world in which we live.

Pursuit of Happiness

THE FRAMERS OF THE United States' Constitution decided that all men had a right to life, liberty, and the pursuit of happiness.

I believe it is very telling that we are not guaranteed happiness, but rather the ability to pursue it. Even they who saw America in its youth, full of promise and opportunity, understood that happiness was not a given.

However, what they and many people fail to realize is that happiness can't be pursued. It can only be lived. You can pursue objects, possessions, even other people. But you can't chase after happiness. Either you have it or you don't. If you don't, and you keep running after it, odds are you've already left it behind when you set off in search of it.

So how do you become happy? The Torah offers a surprising number of insights into this question.

Impulse Buys

*T*HOSE OF US WHO never majored in Marketing in school still know some of the "tricks of the trade," and we are seldom fooled by them. A perfect example is the supermarket. Higher-priced items are placed at eye-level; cheaper, yet just as good, products are placed at floor level where we're not likely to want to bend to get at them. They don't fool us. We might take the more expensive brand but it's because we *choose to*, not just because we can't see bending all the way down for a measly twenty cents.

Another item is the ever-popular "impulse buy." These items, such as candy placed at the register, are things nobody goes to the store for, but few seem to be able to leave without. The idea is that you say to yourself, "I don't need that, but it would be nice...Hey, I work hard, I deserve it...Okay, just two and that's all!" (Well, maybe just one more, in case I drop the first ones.)

We have been trained to know that impulse is bad. Here we are being taken in, and yet we sheepishly go along with it. But we're not fooled! We choose to buy these frivolous items because we truly *want* them. But does it have to be something bad? Why don't they ever put apples at the checkout line? Or those organic sesame soy chips your ovo-vegan-latte sister-in-law is so fond of (now with real alfalfa!)?

Well, maybe someone has put something healthy at the checkout. Recently, I have seen a new "impulse buy" at the registers of some of my local merchants. Unlike the other ones that I quickly slip into the cart, these made me stop and think. Why would they think I "needed" this? Would it be an "impulse buy"?

The "product" was a display with three cards of various denominations, each to be scanned by the checkout person and paid for by me. What were these cards? Donations to *Tomchei Shabbos*.

It is a brilliant idea! At the checkout register, we have already spent a ton of money on ourselves. This is the spot where we turn a blind eye to spending a little more. What better place than here to get us to help someone less fortunate? How easy for us to get some of the spiritual nutrients we so desperately need!

When approached for *tzedakah*, we often analyze the person collecting. Does he look like he needs the money? Where'd he get that fancy coat? Hmmm, I didn't hear him answer *amen* to *Kaddish...* he must be a faker. We use our logical reasoning to discount the truth about *tzedakah*.

R' Akiva was asked why, if Hashem loves poor people, doesn't He give them money? His answer was, "To keep the rest of us out of *Gehinnom*." So it turns out that they're doing *us* a favor by taking the *tzedakah*. How can we reason our way out of it?

When I saw the cards, I had an impulse to buy one. I wasn't fooled; I knew it was put there for that very reason. But that's what was so great about it. Here was something good for me, and it was so easy to do.

Impulse itself isn't a bad thing, it just depends what the impulse is telling us. Next time you get the urge to do something you maybe shouldn't, tell yourself it's just a marketing ploy of the *yetzer hara* to see if you're a sucker. But, if you get the urge to do something good, go ahead and do it. You're not the one being fooled, your *yetzer hara* is.

By the way, there is an easy way to tell if something is a good impulse. The good impulses don't last very long. So take advantage and listen to your impulse. Well, except maybe on the soy chips!

Smiley Faces

Y*OU MAY NEVER HAVE* heard of freelance artist Harvey Ball, but you've almost certainly seen some of his work. In 1963, while working at State Mutual Life Assurance Company, Mr. Ball created a yellow circle with two black ovals for eyes and a curve for a mouth. Behold, the birth of the smiley face!

In 1970, two entrepreneurs capitalized on this logo and placed it on T-shirts, mugs, and other products, often with a slogan like "Have a happy day." The smiley face experienced tremendous growth and spread all over the world. In fact, the phrase "smiley face" has come to mean much more than the ubiquitous yellow orb and is frequently used to show approval, such as on children's school papers and notes.

I frequently pass a certain toll booth which has both Express EZ Pass lanes, where you travel through at 35 miles per hour, and those standard EZ Pass lanes where you have to slow down to 15 MPH and wait for the light to change from yellow to green. On one of those 15 MPH lanes, someone used tape to make a "frown face" on the yellow light, and a "smiley face" on the green one. I often will choose to slow down and use that one, because it makes me feel good to make the face switch from sad to happy.

Why my sudden preoccupation with smiley faces? Recently I was in my children's school and saw several signs in the hallways with the words "*V'hayu einecha ro'os es morecha* — And your eyes should see your teachers." It had pictures of *gedolim* on it, some of which were Sukkos posters. As I looked at the faces of these holy men, one thought struck me: they were scary-looking! Not ONE picture showed them smiling. In each picture, it looked like they were unaware that they were being photographed, had just sneezed, or were trying to figure out what new-fangled dance the *buchurim* were doing at a wedding. Some looked angry, others looked spaced out. NONE of them made me want to get to know them better.

And it's not their fault. For some reason, I assume the photographers and poster makers thought it would be better if the *rabbanim* and *roshei yeshivah* they included did not smile, lest someone take *Yiddishkeit* too lightly — not seriously enough. Personally, I think that is ridiculous.

So many *gedolim* were known for their trademark smiles— R' Shlomo Zalman Auerbach *z"l*, R' Yaakov Kaminetzky *z"l*, R' Avraham Pam *z"l*. If it was so important for people to fear them, they would never have been caught smiling, and yet, they constantly were. When they posed for pictures, they flashed brilliant, welcoming grins which made you want to get to know them.

Even the *Tanna* Shammai, whom we all think of as strict and stern, was the one who said, "Greet each person with a nice face." Clearly, smiling is NOT frowned upon in Judaism. In fact, the *berachah* given to Yehudah, "*Ul'ven shinayim mi'chalav* — And teeth white from milk," is explained to teach us that showing someone the whites of your teeth (i.e. smiling) is better than giving them a nourishing glass of milk to drink.

What does a smiley face mean, and why does it generally make us smile?

I think the secret is that a smile is a mark of approbation. It is directed at us, even in picture form. It looks right at us and says, "You make me happy!" The ability to make someone happy is an instinctive need in all of us. When we coo to a baby and it smiles, we are excited and gratified because it means we did something good. It means we are on the right track. When our child or spouse sees us and smiles, we are elated because we know that to them, just by showing up, we've made them happy. It does wonders for our self-esteem, and we are inspired to do *more* to make them happy.

Now back to the *gedolim* posters. If you ever meet a *tzaddik*, a righteous person, or a *gadol,* you will be greeted with a warm smile. Why? Because they have such *ahavas Yisrael* that they are made happy just by seeing you. They see in you a *tzelem Elokim* (the image of God), i.e., one of His beloved children. They aren't looking at what you haven't done or your failings, they are looking at the *neshamah* you possess and that is enough to make them smile.

When you see them, you are warmed up; you want to do more to make them smile. You want to be a better person. You want to be a better Jew. That's why *Chazal* tell us that we should see our *gedolim* — because we will be inspired to become better. It is the *gedolim* who can see the good in us and inspire more of the same.

And you don't need to be the *Gadol Hador* to do that either. I was in a store one day when I saw a young yeshivah *rebbi* speaking to a teenaged boy with a small *kippah* who was wearing fashionably torn jeans. Clearly, he wasn't part of the yeshivah, but that didn't make a difference. This young *rebbi* always has such a smile of love and joy on his face when he sees another Jew, no matter his background or current status, that people love him; and when he and this young man finished their conversation, they parted with a big hug.

Now tell me, what do you think would have a better effect on this young man: criticizing his taste in clothing and telling him what he should be doing, or flashing him a glowing smile and letting him know how happy you are to see him, a holy Jew?

I know that unfortunately, while most of us know that the

latter is more effective, we are more likely to take the former approach. It's something I struggle with constantly, focusing on the good in others and ignoring the less-than-perfect items. That's why we should look to the great personages of *Klal Yisrael* who treat each Jew with respect, love, and a genuine happiness to see them. By emulating them we can make the world a happier place.

The people who made the posters likely think the sages should look saintly and distant, to remind us how far we are from where we could be, but nothing could be further from the truth. We should think of them smiling, happy to see us because we are beloved by Hashem. Those smiles tell us: "You are wonderful and make Hashem happy. He smiles upon you, and you should smile upon others as well."

The Secret of Happiness

I HAVE OFTEN THOUGHT I would like to write a book in which I would tell people how to solve all their problems, and thus make millions of dollars in royalties while riding on a sea of praise and appreciation from the people whose lives I've bettered. Of course, it is often at those same times that I believe I can fly with the purple ~~hippopotamuses~~ ~~hippopotami~~ ~~hippothalamus~~ *elephants* who are selling cotton candy to the Jolly Green Giant. And then I wake up.

Truly, I would like to help people better their lives, deal with disappointment, control anger, and basically make this world a better place to live — but I can't. You see, there is some pervasive notion that books have to have enough pages so as to be made of a sufficient number of trees to kill a small ecosystem (or at least a relatively well-wooded backyard) in order to be worth buying. Nobody will pay $12.95 for a book that is two pages long with the first page being the one intentionally left blank.

You see, I don't have a lot of advice to give. Despite what the modern world claims we need to be happy, with such memorable mottos as "Indulge yourself," "Giving is its own reward," and "Coke, the Real Thing," I believe the true secret to happiness is much simpler than that. If I had to sum up the secret of happiness, I could do it in two words: "Thank you."

Now, you're probably saying to yourself, "Of course it's important to say thank you, but how can that be the secret to happiness?"

The difference is that I'm not just referring to *saying* "Thank you," I mean you should *live* "Thank you."

This isn't new; this has been the Torah's viewpoint for all time, and it is the hallmark of the Jewish People. The word *Yehudi* (Jew) is from the root of acknowledgment and thanks. Okay, so you still don't see where I'm going, but think about it like this: When we're unhappy, there's nearly always a feeling of something lacking or missing.

"I don't have the house/car/job/children/hair I know I deserve; I deserve better, if only I had..." We make some basic mistakes and they cause our problems. To start, let's clear the air:

YOU DON'T DESERVE ANYTHING — the Master of the World put you here to test your soul, to see if you can face the challenges and choose to serve Him. Everything you get in this world is a bonus, because you did nothing to earn the ability to live, breathe, see, hear, smell, taste, touch, think, waterski or calculate the square root of pi using a slide rule and a can of Budweiser. So, before you say, "I don't have enough," think about thanking God for all that you DO have. You'd be surprised how much you really have to be thankful for when you start listing it (and don't forget about the ability to make that list!).

FATHER KNOWS BEST — Hashem knows exactly what's best for you and that's most often *not* what you think is best. A fellow applied for a job managing the sporting goods department at a local Montgomery Ward department store. Had he not been passed over for the promotion, he likely would not have grown up to be the president of the United States. At least that's how Ronald Reagan saw it. *L'havdil*, another applied for a job as a *rav*, and the community didn't hire him. His family was disappointed, but had he gotten the job, they likely would have remained in Europe and been killed by the Nazis, and R' Yaakov Kamenetsky *z"l* and his family would never have come to America. We make choices, but Hashem is really pulling the strings to get us where we need to be.

PEOPLE LIKE BEING THANKED — Mr. Kramer (not his real name) is a wonderful, friendly man who lives at an assisted-living facility. I met him at the eye-doctor's office one day, when a power-outage cut short our appointments. He didn't have a ride back and I offered to drive him. He was a bit hesitant about my driving skills (though anyone will tell you that I am a relatively good driver, as long as you're not asking my wife). Anyway, I gave him a ride home, and we made pleasant conversation about my cousin in Boston, his children, and my alma mater, Telshe Yeshivah in Cleveland. I dropped him off and figured that was that. It was far from over, though.

A few days later, I received a letter from him, written in long-hand. "In the old days, when I worked at a candy store," he wrote, "I would thank someone who did me a favor by sending them a box of chocolate. I can't do that now, so I tried to think of something else to send. Enclosed are copies of letters I received from R' Dessler *z"l* when I got out of the camps after WWII. I thought you would find them interesting as we discussed my having corresponded with him." WOW.

Here was a fellow who just got a ride from me, spent maybe ten or fifteen minutes in the passenger seat, and he was *sending* me something to thank me! He appreciated that I had given him a ride (something many of us do without giving it much thought) and wanted to show his appreciation so badly that he looked for something that *I* would appreciate! It was a tremendous lesson to me about how much I have to appreciate the things I have and receive.

Mr. Kramer didn't feel like he was owed a ride, though surely others might have expected a young fellow like me to give him the courtesy and respect this *zaken* deserved. He felt grateful to me and showed it. He apparently knows the secret of happiness and shared it with me.

And now, I've shared it with you.

It's High Time We Start Stop-Thinking

S OME YEARS AGO, a bumper sticker and slogan became wildly popular. It was, in truth, one of the dumbest slogans in history. It just shows that if something sounds good, as long as you don't really think about it, it can be successful.

The slogan was, "Practice random acts of kindness and senseless acts of beauty." People around the world got excited about this concept. They figured that along with all the other intellectual and emotional sludge they pour into the environment we call "the world," they would occasionally drop in a spritz of deodorant and make everything alright. Anyone who has ever sat next to someone who is trying to cover up three days of un-showered *shvitz* with extra doses of perfume or cologne will attest that this doesn't work.

You see, when you perform kindness or try to create something beautiful, it can't be random or senseless. If you haven't put in any thought, then the result is potluck. Maybe what you think is beautiful is really repulsive. (The woman who used to eat rugalech with techinah comes to mind…) Maybe your kindness is more senseless than just random.

As Jews, we are commanded to perform kindness constantly, and follow the *Ribono shel Olam*'s sense of beauty. We are told, "Open your hand to your needy brother," "You shall surely bear his burden with him," "Do not antagonize the stranger for you know how he feels," and many similar directives. Our kindness must be calculated and methodical, and above all, NOT random.

When we do mitzvos they should be beautiful. Stealing to get the money for an expensive *esrog* is NOT beautiful; it simply does not make sense. Neither does cheating on your taxes to afford a bigger donation to your *shul* (and the lovely plaque that comes with it).

That's why I'm proposing that everyone reading this article practice a new approach called "Stop-thinking." We all think constantly, and we make decisions based on our thought processes. Are we really making the best decisions possible?

Imagine this scenario: A newspaper delivery boy is riding his bike down the block. At each house, as he is whizzing by, he hurls a paper in the general vicinity of the door. He is lucky if it lands in the same town as the customer. Most often, it ends up through a window, in the rhododendrons, or on the neighbor's paper-mâché bullfight lawn ornaments. What if he had stopped his bike, taken aim, and thrown the paper? I bet he'd be much more accurate and cause many fewer problems.

Now back to our topic. We are rushing through life, making decisions that are much more important than whether the paper lands on the doormat or the matador. I propose that when we are making decisions that affect other people (and which ones don't?) we stop, take aim, and make effective choices.

Let's take some practical examples. Of course, we must start with my old favorite, the shopping cart. You're running late, harried, trying to get out of the store with the nosh you promised your six-year-old for his *chumash* party, as well as the ingredients your wife needs for the recipe she is making *this minute* and the basic necessities you were supposed to pick up yesterday but forgot. And you're trying to do all this in four minutes. As you get back to your car, you throw the stuff in the trunk (not the eggs — you've got to be real careful with eggs...) and you want to head out. What do you do with the shopping cart? If you're whizzing past, you think, "I don't have time to put it away, I'm in a hurry." But, if you stop-think, you might say, "I am in a hurry, but the extra ten seconds won't make that much of a difference, and the next person who wants to pull in may also be in a hurry." Now ask yourself, which one will get you noticed in *Shamayim*? Answer: Both will, but by different sides of the courtroom.

How about conversations? Most people never let thought stand in the way of saying what they want. Saying "what's on your mind" has to be one of the world's greatest oxymorons. If our words had gotten within ten feet of our brains, we likely wouldn't say half the things we do!

Your friend just bought a home. He doesn't have any children even after several years of marriage. Do you "stop-think" and wish him to "fill it with children and *berachah*," or do you whiz along and ask, "Why do you need a house, you don't have any kids?!" I think we all know which one really happened and how the home-buyer felt about his new purchase and his old "friend."

Or, you come home after a busy day and the place is flying. Do you stop-think and realize that something must have caused it and you should see what you can do to help? Or are you more likely to whiz along, self-absorbed, and start yelling about why things aren't put away? Okay, now, which one of these will lead to *shalom bayis* and children with good self-esteem? Was it the one you picked? Mmm-hmm, I thought so.

So, this is my plan. I envision placards and posters reminding people to start "stop-thinking." I encourage people to practice continuous acts of kindness and thoughtful acts of beauty. I can see the signs now. Flyers, posters, business cards... Maybe I'll even make bumper stickers! Well, maybe not. Now that I stop and think about it, they'd probably never sell.

Waive the Crave

A MAN WALKS INTO A bagel store in the midst of a torrential downpour. It is thundering and lightning. Shivering and sopping wet, he asks the man behind the counter for an everything bagel with cream cheese. "What else?" asks the bagel man. "Nothing. My wife just wants an everything bagel with cream cheese."

"You mean your wife sent you here just for a bagel and cream cheese?!"

"Of course," the dripping man replied. "Do you think my *mother* would send me out on a night like this for just a bagel with cream cheese?!"

Of course it's a joke. Most wives wouldn't send their husbands out in a storm for just a bagel and cream cheese. Usually they'd want a Danish, too.

We all know that when a craving hits, it's hard to ignore. All pregnant women can quote verbatim the *halachah* that says if a pregnant woman is craving something she is to eat it, even on Yom Kippur. When faced with that argument, most men might not be able to refuse and will find themselves looking for Ben & Jerry's or dill pickles at 3 A.M. in a part of town that makes you wish you had paid attention in Spanish class.

Not all men have that problem, though. When my sister had a craving, my brother-in-law would say, "I'm in the middle of something. Give me fifteen minutes and if you still want it I'll run out and get it." Brilliant! Of course, fifteen minutes later she wasn't in the mood of what she had wanted anymore, and he rarely had to go out. I think he hit on something.

Often, when something hits us out of the blue, it's a feeling that will pass momentarily. Like, for example, when we have a really good zinger to say to someone. If we blurt it out, we are proud of ourselves for the "good one." Of course, if we waited a few seconds, and perhaps even allowed our brains to process the remark, we might change our minds and hold our tongues.

I remember one day at *Minchah* when a friend leaned over and made a comment to me. I couldn't hear him, but the *chazan* started *Kedushah* and we both focused on our *davening*. After *Minchah*, I walked past him, but he didn't say anything. Apparently, the interruption made him decide that what he had said wasn't worth repeating.

Chazal tell us a person doesn't sin unless a "wind of foolishness" enters him. Okay, so how long do you react to a gust of wind? Usually, if it takes you by surprise, you grab your yarmulke/hat or your *shaitel*/snood/bandana/*tichel* and steady yourself. But if you are heading out and know it's windy, you're better prepared and you don't have to chase any headgear down the block.

In essence, if you can avoid reacting to the initial stimulus, you can nearly always calmly and rationally go about your business. It's when you act impulsively that you get into trouble. Like when the zinger that pops out is about your mother-in-law who happens to be standing right behind you. Or when you make a joke during *davening* and speak at a time it's forbidden to do so.

How about when you see that $150 purse you "just have to have!" (Men, please skip this part and read further. You won't understand it; I know I don't.) If you stop and think, you might realize that you don't have any occasion to use it, it clashes with everything else in your wardrobe, and you just bought a purse a week ago. Plus, that money could be put to much better use on a pair of cute boots.

Another example is when you stub your toe in the dark in the middle of the night. It might initially make sense to yell "ouch!" However, if you stop and think about it, you'll realize that if you do that, you might wake someone up. It's bad enough that you can't go back to sleep, but if that someone is under the age of eighteen, they may decide that it's morning, time to rise and shine, and sing that new song they love at the top of their lungs while jumping on their bed and strumming a hairbrush. Okay, yelling, "Ouch" is a bad idea.

And, if you work on yourself, besides for biting your lip, you might say, "*Zol zein a kaparah.* Thank you Hashem for giving me this punishment instead of something worse." It's amazing how philosophical and deep you can be if you just pause to think before acting.

So, this week's challenge is to "waive the crave." Push back the impulsive actions and deliberate before you do something. Logic and rational thought will prevail!

Not Small Potatoes

*T*HESE ARE TIMES WHICH try men's souls. Money is tight, jobs are hard to come by, and if you have a job, you should be thanking *HaKadosh Baruch Hu* for it. It's easier to pray to keep a job than to pray for a new one after you've lost the one you had.

Well, one young man was looking for work, and a grocer, seeing the boy's honesty and integrity, decided to give him an easy job with good pay. "Your job," said the grocer, "is to sort the potatoes for sale. You put the big potatoes in this bin, and the small potatoes in that bin."

The boy began in earnest but after two days, the boy quit. "I don't understand it," wondered the boss. "Were the potatoes too heavy?"

"No," replied the boy.

"Well, was the pay too low?" queried the grocer.

"Not at all," came the reply.

"So what was it that made you give up an easy job sorting potatoes with good pay?"

"The potatoes were not heavy, and the pay was good. But the decisions were killing me!"

Often, we can feel like the boy in the story. We are constantly faced with questions, dilemmas, challenges, and decisions to be made. We usually know which are the big potatoes, and we can tell which are the small. Those are easy. The question is the medium ones. We don't know how to categorize them and that wears us out.

Having to choose constantly, and second-guessing ourselves, can be draining physically, emotionally, and spiritually. But what if the boss gave the boy a machine that sorted the potatoes for him?

Imagine he had a job sorting potatoes where all he had to do was put the potatoes in the machine and the smaller potatoes fell through a hole into one bin and the larger ones rolled down the track to the large bin? They do it for coins and when you dump a jar full of them into the machine it shakes them around and gives you cash. I bet he'd never give up a cushy job like that, especially with such good pay!

Well, guess what. You are a potato sorter. So am I. We face decisions every day and have to make determinations about what we will do in each situation. Getting tired yet? Don't worry. We have a sorting machine.

That machine is called the Torah and it guides us in making the decisions we face each day. If we had to rely on our own intellect and intuition, we'd get ragged rather quickly. We'd second-guess ourselves after every failure, and after every success we'd question whether we could have done something differently to have even more success.

But not when we have that amazing sorting machine working for us. Now, we take our decisions, and run them through the Torah. If it says we should do it, we do, and know that our success or failure is out of our hands. Just as the grocer couldn't complain that the boy put a big potato in the small bin, or vice versa, because it was his machine that made the determination, so, too, Hashem will have no complaints on us if we follow the Torah and we will get our ample reward.

R' Yosef Chaim Sonnenfeld *z"l* once dreamed he knew the winning lottery numbers. He only had enough money either for bread for that day for his family, or the ticket. He couldn't do both. He said, "Hashem promises to gives us our *parnasah* each day. This money is for that. He will take care of tomorrow."

The numbers came up. Had he bought the ticket he would have had a fortune. Someone asked him if he regretted not having bought the ticket. "Not at all," he replied. "I did the right thing. The rest is up to Hashem."

Can you imagine the equanimity a person has to have to be that blasé about something like that? How many of us would have gone around despondent for weeks, kicking ourselves for not acting upon it, and then spending the next twenty years running after every lottery opportunity and pouring so much money down the drain? Most of us, I'd venture, unless you're using the sorting machine.

The Torah isn't a list of suggestions, or even a "hot tip" on what to choose. It is an actual piece of hardware, designed to accurately measure each question placed in it and respond with the correct answer.

Imagine you are faced with the following dilemma: Someone told you some information about a neighbor. If it is true, he did a horrible thing. You wonder if you should go tell him off. What to do?

Put it in the sorting machine.

Can I believe it? <BEEEEP> Nope. Not allowed to believe *lashon hara*.

Okay, but can I suspect it's true to protect myself? <WHIIIIRRR> Yes. That's okay.

Now, on the chance that it's true should I say, "I heard that you did such-and-such" and try to correct him? <BUUUUUUZZZZZ> No. That could lead to *rechilus* if you mention who told you but what you can do is…

And so on down the line it goes. Do I take this job where the people use foul language or I have to do dishonest things? <ZIIIPP> No, Hashem can provide for you in an honest and proper way. No need to sully yourself.

Can you eat this food? <CHUKA-CHUKA> Sorry, Hashem said no.

Now, why *should* you listen to the machine? Because it's good for you. If you make a decision on your own and it's wrong, you will pay the price. The Torah has given us rules for many reasons, but one of them is because the world was set up in such a way that if you follow them you'll be healthy and strong, but if you don't, get ready for spiritual swine flu which most often presents with physical symptoms as well.

And no, you don't get paid extra if you make the right decision on your own. Even if you are lucky enough to make the right call, you've been foolish because you took a chance of erring when the Boss gave you all the tools you needed.

Of course, sometimes He throws in tests. He wants to see if you will use the machine properly or just follow your own feelings on the matter. That's dangerous. Someone could lose an eye! If we follow our own feelings instead of the Torah's guidelines, the results will be disastrous and we will regret it. Maybe not today; maybe not tomorrow. But someday, and for the rest of our lives… and beyond.

The truth is that having this machine called Torah makes life pleasant and peaceful. You will never again have to wonder whether you made the wrong decision and you can go to an expert sorter for advice and help. Best of all, you will always be able to be confident that you will enjoy a cushy job where you don't have to make tough decisions and at the end of the day you are sure to get your pay with bonuses. And that's no small potatoes.

You Can't Always Get What You Want

(But If You Try, Sometimes, You Can Want What You Get)

Y EARS AGO I HEARD someone say, "When I was a kid, I prayed to God to send me a bike. I prayed and prayed, but nothing happened. I realized God doesn't work that way. So I stole one, and asked Him to forgive me."

Obviously, while funny, that's not the way to go about things. It's a basic concept of *Yiddishkeit* that while we may not get what we want, we always get what we need. So, if we're supposed to get the bike (or car, or house, or job, or appreciation, or money, or recognition) we will get it in God's time, not our own, and there's no need to break any rules to try to get it.

Of course, *davening* is an important first step. When the world was created, all the growing things were hovering just below the surface, waiting for rain. The rain was waiting for the *tefillos* of Adam HaRishon. The power of *tefillah* to bring things to fruition is inherent in the world and we should use that tool as much as possible. Sometimes, though, like our friend discovered, you don't get what you *daven* for. What then?

Well, at a certain point, we have to understand that it's simply not good for us to get what we're asking for. This past Shavuos, it was so hot that it was almost unbearable. I kept *davening* to

Hashem that it get cooler. "Please let it cool down"; "*Ribono shel Olam*, please make it cooler"; "even just ninety would be better." To no avail.

Then something hit me. I think it was sunstroke. Just kidding. Actually, I had a thought and changed my *tefillah*. "*Ribono shel Olam*," I said, "for whatever reason, You want it to be hot. Please help us to enjoy the heat." It's amazing how fulfilled I felt after that prayer. I wasn't comfortable, but at least I knew that I was asking for something that was on target, and could be achieved without any miracles.

The heat seemed to bother me less after that, and I accepted it happily, albeit with a greater appreciation for air conditioning.

In *Pirkei Avos*, Rabban Gamliel, son of R' Yehudah HaNasi tells us: Treat [Hashem's] will as if it were your own, so that He should treat your will as if it were His will. Essentially, if you subjugate your will, He will do the same. The basic understanding is that one should devote as much time and money to mitzvos as he does to his own desires. In return, Hashem will help him beyond all expectations. It becomes a *middah k'neged middah* (measure for measure) situation. Since Hashem sees that you are doing what's important to Him, He does what's important to you.

I suggest there is another explanation. If we keep looking for our desires to be fulfilled, often we will meet with disappointment. Most depression in the world comes from unfulfilled expectations. We expect life to be pain-free and it's not. We expect everyone to like us and they don't. We expect to get all the things we want and often fail. That's probably why the founding fathers of the United States said that everyone was entitled to life, liberty, and *the pursuit* of happiness. As long as happiness is outside yourself, based on things beyond your control, you can only pursue it. However, if your happiness is internal, you possess it. So how do you do that?

One way is by changing your desires so that you want whatever Hashem wants to give you. When you remind yourself constantly that God ultimately determines what you will get, and that He will not give you things that are bad for you, you can start to be happy with what He gives you.

Therefore, we can explain the Mishnah in *Avos* as follows: "Make Hashem's will your own," want what He wants; "so that your will shall be done when His is done" and you will always get your way.

When you stub your toe, catch your breath, then say "*Baruch Hashem*," and appreciate that you got something that was coming to you in a relatively benign way. When you don't get something you really want, remind yourself that if Hashem doesn't want you to have it, you don't want it! It wouldn't be good for you, so be happy you were spared.

To end off, I'd like to recount a story I heard from R' Yisrael Reisman which brings out this point.

A man visited an insane asylum and when he entered one room, he found an inmate staring blankly at the wall and moaning, "Nechama'le, Nechama'le, how could you do this to me Nechama'le?" The guest asked the nurse for an explanation. "At one time," she said, "this fellow dated a woman named Nechama'le. He really wanted to marry her but she left him and married someone else. He lost it, and has been doing this ever since."

A bit down the hall, they came to another room. Here, too, the man was moaning, "Nechama'le, Nechama'le, how could you do this to me Nechama'le?" Taken aback at this woman's impact, the visitor asked, "What happened, did she dump him too?"

"No," replied the nurse. "That's the guy she married."

Why Are Yawns Contagious?

*H*AVE YOU EVER SEEN someone yawn across the room? It starts with a somewhat tense look on their face, then their mouth begins to open until they look like a hippo at the zoo, or a seal at feeding time. Sometimes they won't even attempt to cover their mouths, so they look somewhat like human manholes sans the covers. I had a *rebbi* in eighth grade who used to say, "*Harchev picha v'amaleihu* — Open your mouth and I will fill it," when a boy was rude enough to yawn without covering his mouth.

But I'm not writing about the people who are yawning, I'm writing about the results. I know that since I started writing this piece, describing someone yawning, I myself have yawned at least five times. Did you ever notice how yawns seem to be contagious? When you see someone yawn, almost inevitably you begin to yawn as well. The weird thing is, nobody can explain it.

Now, I don't think we can explain yawns at all, and that's the first issue. I used to think it was your body's way of getting extra oxygen, but I think I made that up and it's bogus. As far as I know, scientists have not come up with an explanation for why we yawn. However, an even more perplexing question is why yawns seem to travel from person to person.

I recall reading about a contest for the most unanswerable question. I believe the question of "Why are yawns contagious?" beat out hundreds of other entries to take the prestigious second place. [First place went to: Why can't you tickle yourself?]

Personally, the tickle question seems to me to at least have a possible answer since you yourself know where you're going to touch so the sensation is not a surprise, but the catching yawns thing really has me. (By the way, nearly every time I write the word "yawn," I seem to have to yawn!)

This thought crossed my mind during *davening* one day, when I saw a fellow yawn on the other side of shul and I convinced myself that I wasn't going to... going to... YYYYAAAAWWWWNNNNN... ohhh, excuse me!

I wondered why we yawn, and why it's catching, and why nobody can come up with an answer for it. There may not be an answer for the first two, but perhaps the answer to why we can't come up with an answer is just that — because some things are meant to be unanswerable.

A few nights before I wrote this piece, I spoke with a friend who was going through a rough time. He couldn't understand why Hashem was doing these things to him. I couldn't help him with those answers, but I tried to reassure him that an answer exists, because everything Hashem does is for a reason, and usually we see the good afterwards.

Now, my Philosophy of the Yawn was telling me that people can live without answers, understanding that it's the nature of the world. We don't know why yawns are catchy, or what purpose that serves, but we know that God designed the world for that to happen, so we accept it.

Maybe Hashem chose something as silly as a yawn to give us an inkling about things that are much more serious. We all accept that we will yawn and it doesn't make us question the Divine origins of the universe, nor do we wonder about Hashem's daily involvement in our lives because of it.

Nothing about the yawn awakens uncertainties within us, and we're fine with not knowing why. In fact, we might think it silly to obsess about it. If we extrapolate that, we might realize that when we see little children hysterical because their cookie fell on the floor, we also see that as an overreaction. It's not the end of the world, even if at that moment, from their perspective, everything is crumbling around them (no pun intended).

Or when a teenager gets a breakout and their face looks like something you ordered with extra cheese and olives, you know that it's just temporary and they will manage to grow up somehow. Like the yawn, it seems silly to obsess over something transient.

Now, when we go through difficult situations, perhaps we can think of the same thing. When we catch a yawn, it doesn't bother us that something happened beyond our control. When we see a child throwing a tantrum over silliness, we feel bad for him because he doesn't see the truth.

When we experience hardships we also need to understand that Hashem has a reason for it and it's just temporary. Even if it's a serious illness *Rachmana litzlan,* this whole world is just a passing phase for our *neshamos.*

Interestingly, we yawn most when we're tired. When we go through stress, we also get tired and run down and feel we can't cope. Perhaps that's why Hashem sends us the message at those times, "I'm in control, don't worry about it."

Maybe yawning is a mystery and it's just another unanswerable question, but now, I don't think I'll let it bother me anymore. And the next time things seem so awful you can't take it, take a nap and send your *neshamah* to its source. It will come back rejuvenated, and you will see that sometimes you don't really need to know all the answers.

When I Grow Up, I Want to Be in Chinuch

WHEN WE'RE CHILDREN, PEOPLE always ask us, "What do you want to be when you grow up?" While they mean well, that's like asking a blind man, "What time is it on that sundial?" He hasn't got a clue, or the tools to give you a rational answer.

Yes, perhaps we want them to know they can be anything, but really, how many firefighter policeman astronauts do the New York Yankees need playing shortstop?

I think the question should be asked later. Many agree. They wait until the child is in high school to start to figure out what profession they will choose. That determines the next step. If they go to college, law school, or medical school based on this decision, they are closer to choosing, but I still think that's premature. I have seen many people go to college for one thing, then never actually work in that field, or work in it for a short time then end up doing something else.

You see, I don't think people can really determine what they want to be until they decide WHO they want to be. Yes, you can be a computer programmer, but if you don't get a lift out of it, how enjoyable will it be? Maybe you're a people person, and driving a taxi would suit you better. Now, before anyone tries to point out the fiduciary differences between the two, may I remind you that we believe *HaKadosh Baruch Hu* determines *parnasah*, and we just work because He said we should. People don't become lawyers because lawyers can make a lot of money. Lawyers can make a lot of money because Hashem wants people who are supposed to get money to make money in a "natural" way.

There's a cynical expression, "Those who can — do, those who can't — teach." The Jewish corollary to that is that someone who "can't cut it" in the "real world" goes into *Chinuch*. How sad it is when people think this way. I have a friend who was actually preparing for law school when someone asked him if he believed that Hashem dictates *parnasah*. When he replied in the affirmative, he was asked, "Why not go into *Chinuch*? You think the world needs another lawyer?" *Baruch Hashem*, he did, and I can't tell you how many *talmidim*'s lives he has affected. I can also tell you that the level of honor and respect he enjoys from the people who know him is greater than any lawyer gets.

Now, I'm not here to bash lawyers (well, maybe except for a few of you — you know who you are). I'm here to say that teaching people Torah is probably the highest vocation to which one can aspire.

For months, when anyone asked my three-year-old daughter what she wanted to be, her answer was "a doctor for babies." Of course that made us proud. She loved babies, and wanted to make a career of helping them. Such *Yiddishe nachas*!

Lately, however, now that she's turned four, she responds that she wants to be a Mommy. "How about a Mommy *and* a doctor, sweetie?" No dice. She just wants to be a Mommy. So much for a higher calling. Or is it?

Let's face it, why were we proud she wanted to be a doctor? Because she loved babies? Because she could find original and amusing uses for Vaseline and a thermometer? I can't speak for my wife, but I think that I was thinking about the prestige, money, and elitist factor that I am frequently railing against in my articles and *divrei Torah*. (What? You're not on my e-mail list for *divrei*

Torah? E-mail subscribe to info@jewishspeechwriter.com today!)

If I think about it rationally, through the prism of Torah, is it really so different? She loves babies and wants to help them. True, as a doctor she could help many different babies, but as a parent she could deeply and meaningfully affect the lives of her children, and shower all that love upon them. She could instill Torah and love of Hashem in them and help them create lives dedicated to helping others as well. Now THAT'S a higher calling.

So, what do I want to be when I grow up? Well, it's hard to say. Of course, a *talmid chacham* and an *eved Hashem*, hopefully, someday. But what about my occupation? What do I want to fill my time with?

When people ask me what I do, I don't mention my day job. I discuss my writing. I tell them I'm a *marbitz Torah*. My focus is helping people find happiness in this world and passage to the next. I write speeches for people because it's such a shame to see a *simchah* go by with food, flowers, and fanfare, but nothing for the *neshamah*. People get up to speak and make corny jokes to get a quick laugh. I write speeches that make people think and want to do something a little better, a little holier. It enhances the *simchah* because it raises the *gashmius* to the level of *ruchnius*. That's why I like writing speeches, to bring holiness to the world and help people see the beauty of Torah.

So, I guess, on the whole, I'd rather be in *Chinuch*. That doesn't mean I'll start teaching *alef-beis* or giving a *blatt shiur*. It means I'll live my life as an example to teach others how to be the best they can be. Whether those others are people who read my articles or hear my speeches, or they're my children, friends, and co-workers, I can be a good teacher. We all can.

So tell me, does the world need another lawyer, or perhaps, is it more important to have another person involved in *Chinuch*? Now ask yourself: what do YOU want to be when you grow up?

JACKPOT!

A NEIGHBOR CALLED THIS EVENING and mentioned that someone in Rockland County had won part of the lottery. Did I buy a ticket she asked? I did and when I checked the numbers, I saw that I had won. Two dollars! I told her that even if I had won the big prize, I didn't think I'd be jumping up and down and whooping for joy. She was incredulous, but to me it seems sort of obvious.

It's just as easy for *HaKadosh Baruch Hu* to make me get the winning numbers as anyone else, and it would just mean I have a new set of goals and tests about what I'd do with the money. It's not like I did anything especially meaningful to win, so why take credit? Not only that, who's to say the money will make me happy? There are plenty of stories of people striking it rich and enduring suffering and pain until disastrous results ensue.

When you have the money, you have to hope you will do the right things with it, not waste it on trivial things or self-gratification. That's a bit daunting. In fact, the whooping it up would be better *after* the money was spent, and you can pinpoint that it went for the right things. It's like buying something or getting married. You hope that you will find happiness and success in what you're investing in, but you never know until the end of the story.

So what would I get excited about? Well, here's one thing I got excited about recently:

A few weeks ago, I wrote an article about counting the *berachos* in *Shemoneh Esreh* on our fingers, so the physical action of flexing will wake us from our reveries and get our minds back on the *tefillah*. A couple of days later, a *rebbi* in a yeshivah came over to thank me. "*Yasher koach* on your article," he said. "I've been trying to think of a solution for years and your idea really works!" I was floored; I was shocked; I was whooping with joy. (Inside, of course. On the surface I just smiled and played it cool.)

When I thought about it, it was amazing. Here was someone who teaches Torah to a number of *talmidim*. If he has a better *Shemoneh Esreh*, he will be a better *rebbi*. That will lead to better Torah study by the *talmidim*, as well as the inculcation of better *middos*. They will lead better lives and do countless more mitzvos, and inspire and teach even more people. It's never-ending income from one idea! — JACKPOT!

R' Meir Shapiro wanted *Klal Yisrael* to be on the same page, literally, and came up with the idea for *Daf Yomi*. In the eighty-five years since he introduced the idea, hundreds of thousands of Jews have studied millions of pages of *Shas*, and he gets credit for every one! Would even the most materialistic of us trade that for a lottery win?

Now, we may not inspire the learning of millions of *dapim*, and we might not give rise to the next *gadol hador*. But what we can do is think about what we're spending our money on and ask whether we're investing in a "lottery win" or a "*siyum haShas*" — a potential possibility of happiness or a surefire immediate spiritual benefit.

We can also think about what we can do to inspire ourselves and others and help them rise in their Torah observance and love of Hashem. Maybe a smile, a caring remark, a cup of coffee when it's needed, or keeping our *tefillin* on until the end of *davening*, can change the course of someone's life, and ultimately the whole world. These chances come up all the time, and we may not even be aware that it's happening.

That's bigger than winning the Mega-millions and more power ful than winning the Powerball. As my wife's Zeidy Shmelka says when he looks at the generations of *frum* children, grandchildren, and great-grandchildren he produced after surviving the Holocaust: "Can you buy that for money?"

Simchah Gedolah
L'hiyos B'Mitzvah

WHEN I WAS IN yeshivah, *shalosh seudos* was often rather a depressing affair. The dining room lights were on a timer so not all of them were on, food was limited to quick-sogging Krispie Rice (*Now pastier than ever!*) some kokosh cake, and some gefilte fish.

The *Rosh HaYeshivah* R' Mordecai Gifter *z"l* didn't come to join us often so when he did come once, the *Rosh Yeshivah* R' Chaim Stein *shlit"a* wanted to impress him with how nice it was. Leaning over to the *bachur* who led the *zemiros*, he said, within earshot of R' Gifter, "*Zingt der lebedike Baruch Keil Elyon* — Sing the lively tune for Baruch Keil Elyon."

Perhaps out of habit, the *bachur* started singing, "*Baaaaaaruuuuuuuucchhh, Keil Elllll-yon, Asher nasan, me-e-nuchah...*" Now if you don't know what I mean, think of a tune that would probably be a popular favorite on the funeral circuit of Eastern Europe in the mid-1800's. Ah... now you've got it.

Anyway, so he told the *bachur* to sing the lively tune and this is what he got instead. With his characteristically sharp wit, R' Gifter said to R' Chaim, "*Tishah B'Av bei dir iz mistomeh a yontif* — [If that's your idea of lively] Tishah B'Av is likely a *Yom Tov* to you."

How many times has this happened to you? You're at a *simchah* and one of the *baal simchah*'s family members is invited to *daven*. He gets up, and with his melodious voice, proceeds to sing the most somber, slow tunes he can think of. What happened to bouncy *niggunim* that have people singing along with smiles on their faces? Why must we always be so serious? Maybe people are supposed to be solemn in a church, but we Jews are told, "*Ivdu es Hashem b'simchah!* — Serve Hashem with happiness!"

I remember one *Shabbos Chazon* in camp. That's the Shabbos before Tishah B'Av when much of the world has the custom to sing *Lecha Dodi* to the solemn tune of *Ali Tzion*, to show some awareness of the upcoming day of mourning. The head counselors were discussing with the *manhig ruchni* whether they had to keep that custom in camp. They determined that for the first part they would, but insisted that the *shaliach tzibbur* pick a lively tune for the second part (It was *Ze-e-eh HaOis asher sahm kail*, for those who are interested.)

Why did they do that? Because they were dealing with youngsters who need to associate *Yiddishkeit* with joy and *simchah* so as they grow older they will be able to find the real, internal, joy for themselves. R' Moshe Feinstein *z"l* was once asked: "So many people came to this country in the early 20th century and sacrificed everything for Shabbos. How is it that their children abandoned it?"

R' Moshe answered, "Because you cannot transmit *mesiras nefesh* (self-sacrifice), you can only transmit *simchah*." The ones who lost their jobs and sighed, "*Oy, s'iz shver tzu zein a Yid — Oy*, it's so hard to be a Jew" were the ones whose children thought, "Who needs it?"

The ones who lost their jobs and said, "*Baruch Hashem* I was *zocheh* to do the *ratzon Hashem*, and protect Shabbos," and rejoiced with their children, those were the ones whose children remained firm and grew up to find the beauty and joy in Shabbos.

Let me share two more stories and then I'll wrap it up.

A man came to my door one afternoon, collecting for a

yeshivah that works with boys with learning difficulties. I had already more than fulfilled my *ma'aser* obligations and was figuring on giving him a modest donation. He asked me for an amount I deemed presumptuous, and also for a post-dated check, for a few months later, something I *never* do. I was stunned by his audacity, but then something else struck me — his *simchas hachaim* (*joie de vivre*).

He told me a vort; he smiled; we shared a joke; he was almost bubbly, excitedly showing me letters and pictures and telling me how they try to give the boys an excitement and *geshmak* in Torah and in life. I thought, "This is a man who can get through to these boys, and is exactly what people need." He reminded me of the Gemara in *Taanis* (22a) wherein R' Broka was in the marketplace with Eliyahu haNavi and asked him if anyone there was a *ben Olam HaBa*, (a person who was certain to receive a portion in the next world).

Eliyahu pointed out two fellows. R' Broka asked them what they did. They responded, "We are jokers, and when we see people who are depressed, we cheer them up." Rashi says, "Jokers: They are *b'simchah* and make others *b'simchah*." I don't recall where I heard this (I'm thinking it was R' Paysach Krohn but I could be wrong), but someone said, "You see? If you want to make someone else happy, you need to be happy yourself." In other words, if you want to help other people find the joy in *Yiddishkeit*, you need to find it yourself. I ended up giving a larger donation than I planned, *and* a post-dated check. I can only *daven* that he is successful, but the fact that he finds *simchah* in being a *Yid* is already a great start.

In *Chovos HaLevavos*, Rabbeinu Bachya says that one of the primary benefits to having *bitachon* is the cessation of worry. Imagine if you honestly and whole-heartedly believed that everything came from *HaKadosh Baruch Hu* and that *hishtadlus* is just for show (as the Chovos HaLevavos says). You'd be able to handle anything that came your way.

I know such a person, and here's a story he told me. He brokered a business deal where his commission was going to be about ten thousand dollars! He did the deal and after waiting four months for this much-awaited amount, he received a letter informing him that the deal turned out to be far less lucrative than he calculated and instead of $10,000, he got $800.

Wow! Can you imagine how disappointed and upset he must have been? To be expecting a huge windfall and wind up with less than 10% of it?! I bet you can't imagine, because he wasn't even fazed. He said, "*Baruch Hashem*, it's meant to be." That's it. Calm, collected, happy. And that's what being a Jew is all about.

One Percent Inspiration

THOMAS EDISON IS CREDITED with saying that a good invention is one percent inspiration, and ninety-nine percent perspiration. If you want to be successful, he means, it's not enough to have a good idea; you have to work hard too.

The second problem with inventing is that you don't usually get your invention called by your name. We don't call it the electric Edison (lightbulb), the Alexander Graham Bell-ephone (telephone), or the Edwin Moore (august inventor of the push-pin.)

Of course, one man managed to defy both of these rules. His name was Charles Ponzi and the Ponzi scheme became the common term for a scheme in which people expected to get rich quickly and which promised investors high returns in a very short time.

For almost a year he rode high, taking in $15 million ($140 million in today's money) and paying out a lot of money to his investors, which came from new investors. In the end, most of them lost a bundle.

My great-Bubby, Vita Kamin *a"h* used to say, "With my own ten fingers I can't make any money. But with someone else's fingers? No problem." She was a smart businesswoman who was one of the first to buy real estate in a little town called Miami Beach, on a street called Collins Avenue. (Unfortunately, the family sold out before we struck it rich, but *gam zu l'tovah*.)

The Ponzi scheme was a take-off from the idea of a pyramid

scheme. In that scenario, I bring in some people below me, they bring in people, who bring in people, and eventually, I have a huge amount of people in my "downline" earning money for me, and I don't have to do the hard work. The reason such programs are illegal is that there are not enough people to keep joining, nor enough money to pay them all.

One day, as I was discussing the outcome of something I had done, and how I had positively influenced some people, it hit me. There was a possible workable program. The ULTIMATE pyramid scheme!

You see, the problem, as I said, was that there was a finite limit to who and what could be earned. Find a way around that minor problem and you've got a working pyramid!

So, what is this workaround? It's simple. Have God as your backer.

Let's say I write something that affects five people. They begin to *daven* better, think more about their *neshamos*, or be nicer to others. Every time they do something good because of my influence, I get credit in *Shamayim*. Now, say they pass along what I've said, or something they came up with after that intense *tefillah*, and it has a positive effect on five other people. They get credit for what they've done, BUT SO DO I! My downline has now increased to twenty-five people doing mitzvos, and I haven't done anything more than my original writing! It keeps continuing, and I get a huge return on my "inspiration."

All the good that happens because of me gets credited to my account. If I was nice to someone and they were nice to someone else, if I cheered them up and they accomplished something worthwhile, if I encouraged them and they cured cancer, my ledger book shows all those huge deposits.

It's brilliant! The more mitzvos I do that inspire others to be greater than they were before, the more I'm racking up the points upstairs. But, in order to make this a success, I want to be sure to maximize how many people participate. That's why I'm writing here. By spreading this concept, I inspire people to "get *sechar* quick" and further my "Jon's-i" scheme.

So, all you have to do is go out and do something nice for someone else. Teach them Torah, help them out, guide them on the *derech Hashem*, and you will start your own downline. It can't fail!

Unfortunately, there is one caveat. True, if you inspire someone to do good you get credit for all the good that comes out of it no matter how many generations or iterations it goes through. However, if you treat someone poorly, tell him or her *lashon hara*, or motivate him to sin, and he passes THAT along — it very likely works the same way.

Ouch.

Holiday
Observances

ANYONE CAN TELL YOU that as Jews, our lives revolve around the holidays of the year. In fact, sometimes one can get dizzy from it.

We have happy days, sad days, solemn days, and silly days. We have days upon which we work, and days upon which we don't. Some holidays need less preparation, and some need months of strategic planning and troop movements.

At the end of the day (or week), however, the point is that we commune with Hashem and find holiness and meaning in every day.

Purim: Variations on a Theme

P URIM IS A TIME for joy, a time for merriment, a time to ask
yourself — what's your theme? Theme? What do you mean
my theme?

Unless you've been living under a rock for the past twenty
years, you undoubtedly know what I'm talking about. You need
to have a theme for Purim. In the past, your *shalach manos* only
required two food items, preferably to be used as part of a *seudah*.
Not anymore!

Now, you need a unifying concept for why those things
go together. It should be something like: "Breakfast" in which
items look like eggs or pancakes, there's a bagel or two and some
cream cheese, and maybe a container of orange juice. It could be
"Noach's *teivah*," and you could include animal crackers, rainbow
Twizzlers and bottles of water. (Bonus points if you dress up like
a six-hundred-year-old man who hasn't showered in months.) Or
it could be something really fun like "Words that begin with R,"
wherein every item in the basket starts with an L. (It's a Purim
shtick, get it?!)

In fact, if your theme is good enough, you don't even need to
have two food items or be able to use it for the *seudah*. If the items
fit your theme well enough, they don't even have to be food. The
main thing is how cutesy it is and how brilliant people will think
you are for coming up with it.

When I was in yeshivah, poems were all the rage. You couldn't send out a *shalach manos* without a poem. That wasn't right! One of the *kollel* fellows even asked me to write one for him because his wife couldn't and was too embarrassed to send out *shalach manos* without it.

I've got a great idea for a theme. How about "Friendship"? In this *shalach manos,* there wouldn't necessarily be smiley face candies or happy little boats. In fact, it wouldn't matter what you put in them, as long as you did it with a glad heart and warm feelings towards the recipient.

This *shalach manos* might be accompanied by a physical delivery, instead of being dropped on the doorstep so you could run to deliver the rest of your *shalach manos* to the people who will be offended if they don't get. More on that in a minute. My "Friendship" *shalach manos* might find you taking a moment to say a pleasant word to someone or writing a personalized note acknowledging their friendship. It might actually make people feel special and loved. The focus wouldn't be on the clever giver, but on the appreciated recipient. Now *that* would be a surprise!

The best line I ever heard about *shalach manos* came from R' Moshe Meir Weiss *shlit"a* of Staten Island. "Make a list of everyone you want to give *shalach manos* to," he said, "then throw that away and give to the people who didn't make it onto your list."

Every *shalach manos* should have friendship as its underlying theme. There shouldn't be a pressure to perform or hurt feelings if you don't get from someone. Can you imagine that when my daughter gave *shalach manos* to her friend, a parent said to my wife, "So now that our kids are friends, WE don't get *shalach manos*?"

If you didn't get *shalach manos* maybe it's because we love you so much that there's no way we could improve the relationship. And if you got offended for not getting the few pieces of candy or wafers in the basket, is there really anything we *could* do to improve the relationship?

Yes, I think we place too much emphasis on overt themes and

too little on the subtle, behind-the-scenes ones. This, of course, is really apropos for Purim. The *Megillah* itself has a recurring theme running through it, which is obvious to us, but the people who lived through it didn't see it.

When Mordechai told the Jews of Shushan not to attend Achashveirosh's feast, they thought it was political suicide, and many ignored his guidance. They seemed to be right for nine years, until Haman's ascendancy to power. Then, their "good" relationship with the king couldn't help them.

It took the machinations of *HaKadosh Baruch Hu* to ensure Esther's rise to power and Mordechai's honor by a wicked king to eventually save the day. To us, looking back, we see the theme of Jews sinning, threats, *teshuvah,* and salvation. But that's perhaps a more overt theme of the Megillah.

Behind the scenes, the real theme was Hashem's actions. Not just hidden from view, but consistent, constant, and continuously moving in the same direction. From the beginning, Hashem was setting the stage for us to be reinvigorated, to accept the Torah not anew, but as a re-acceptance of what we had previously accepted at *Har Sinai.*

The real theme of Purim, therefore, is that all our actions, all our endeavors and behaviors should conform to the single, unified concept that we are the bearers of the Torah, the banner that identifies us as special, connected individuals to the Creator. When all the masquerading is gone and the masks have been removed, our true images must be revealed to show consistent dedication to Hashem and His Torah, as we did at Sinai, and as we did again in Shushan.

If we approach *shalach manos* and the other mitzvos of Purim with that in mind, we will not feel pressured to compete but proud and privileged to fit into the Theme of Creation.

Purim: The Joy of Purim

*A*S I WALKED DOWN the aisles of my local neighborhood grocery store one February afternoon, something hit me. It was almost Purim! Now, when I was in yeshivah, we knew how many months, weeks, days, and hours there were until Purim from about the middle of Elul *zman*.

We had plans to make, ideas to work on and things to do before that wondrous day. Many boys perhaps look forward to it for the almost free-for-all atmosphere of being able to drink until they are no longer able to tell the difference between *baruch* Mordechai and *arur* Haman, or between up and down, or the Yankees and the Mets. Some are *machmir* to drink until they're not even sure whether their feet are actually attached to their bodies, or if that's why they have to tie their shoes, to make sure everything stays connected.

For many of us, however, Purim revolved around collecting for *tzedakah*. Now, while that sounds like a noble cause, I can speak for myself at least that the collecting was merely a way to be able to rent a car, a costume, and then compare who had the biggest haul when you came back.

For some of us, the responsibilities were greater as we arranged the food, music, cars, costume rental (and cleaning afterwards — trust me, you don't want to know). We held onto money, rarely got to drink, and basically didn't get to "enjoy" Purim like everyone else.

What does this all have to do with my revelation in the supermarket? Not much. It just made me think about how priorities change and what seems so important one day can seem insignificant the next. If I were given the opportunity today to get dressed up and spend my whole Purim getting in and out of a car with a drunk pirate or an orangutan leaning on me and singing at the top of his lungs with breath that should not be allowed near an open flame, I daresay I'd pass. Even if it was for a good cause.

You see, as I've grown up, I've learned that Purim is about more than just dancing and streamers and physical excesses. In fact, I'm not even sure those are even part of Purim.

What I have learned is that Purim is a time for a new *kabalas haTorah*. It's a time for powerful *tefillos* that will be answered. I have so many stories of things I've *davened* for, really *davened* for, on Purim, which have come to be. But while so many of us are busy with *shalach manos* themes and seeing how many fifths it takes to make one whole, how much emphasis do we put on *davening* at this auspicious time?

Normally, while my wife and children are delivering *shalach manos,* I try to sit down and learn. If the weather is nice enough, I do it outside my front door. Last year, someone said to me, "Wow, you're the first person I've seen learning today." Is that how it should be?

Yes, there is a wonderful thing called Yeshivas Mordechai Ha-Tzaddik where boys around the world set aside an hour or two to learn at various shuls on Purim morning. But do we plan for that? Is that part of our excitement and anticipation for the upcoming Purim?

If we were saved from annihilation, shouldn't at least part of our celebration revolve around our spiritual salvation instead of just the physical one? Now don't get me wrong, there are many, many Jews who already have the right understanding of what

Purim is and should be. They find the spiritual delights of the *Yom Tov* and use them to elevate the mundane, which is the hallmark of *Yiddishkeit.*

However, there are also a number of Jews who, like me, would otherwise be caught off-guard when Purim shows up. Believe me, more than the celebrations of my yeshivah days required preparation for Purim, to be able to appreciate and properly use all that Purim has to offer needs preparation of mind, body, and soul.

Maybe for next Purim I will try to learn a small *mesechta* to make a *siyum*. Maybe I will plan a *seder* with a *chavrusa* for that morning or figure out some other way to show that Amalek has NOT succeeded in cooling off our burning love for the Torah. Maybe I'll just look forward to the spiritual high I can get and not just the one that comes in a bottle. And maybe, just maybe, I will be able to get a glimpse behind the mask and realize just how involved *HaKadosh Baruch Hu* is in my life everyday. That would definitely be reason to celebrate.

Pesach: What Kind of Jew Are You?

WHILE GOING THROUGH MY daughter's schoolbag, I was struck by a picture she had brought home depicting the four sons mentioned in the Haggadah. It was the stereotypical representation, showing the boys to look something like this:

חָכָם   רָשָׁע   תָּם   שֶׁאֵינוֹ יוֹדֵעַ לִשְׁאוֹל

It hit me that it is rarely as simple as that. If the people who look righteous and studious were always *chachamim*, and every *rasha* looked like a street thug, life would be much easier. The person who hasn't learned how to ask a question (and accept an answer) may not be three, but seventy-three, and people can be totally clueless at any age.

In a sense, the four sons can't be depicted in any particular way because appearance doesn't necessarily tell you what's inside.

I remember traveling one summer and stopping at a take-out store where two *chassidim* were learning *daf yomi*. "They're learning wrong *peshat*," my traveling companion whispered to me, "they misunderstand the Gemara."

"So why don't you tell them?" I asked innocently.

"Look at me," he said, pointing to his khaki pants and polo shirt. "Do you really think they would listen to someone dressed like this?" It is sad but true. We tend to look at people and determine who they are by how they look.

How many people on the way to becoming Torah-observant decided to pack it in since the people they were trying to emulate wrote them off as "not our kind of people" simply because they didn't look like everyone else? Maybe they found more welcoming arms somewhere else. Maybe they stopped wanting to move higher because they didn't like what it looked like "at the top."

How many people have we seen who look like righteous individuals, perhaps even to themselves, who are careless in how they treat others, even earning the Torah's designation "*rasha*" in the process?

There are probably plenty of people who look like they know what's going on, keep mitzvos and appear as fully functioning Jews, yet would love someone to open a dialogue with them and give them a chance to learn and really understand what it's all about.

So what's the answer? How do we determine who someone really is? The *Haggadah* tells us: *by listening.* We are directed to differentiate the four sons by what they say (or don't say). However, even this is not something we can gauge at a glance.

For example, the *rasha* is often depicted as saying, "What's it to you?" He excludes himself and shows he doesn't see the Torah as his. If we look at his words, however, we'll see something interesting. He says, "What is this service to you?" In the Torah, this is exactly the phrase it says our sons will use when asking us about leaving Egypt. Why, then, do we call him a *rasha*? He's perfect!

The answer is that it's *too* perfect. On the surface he's asking just what he should. Only by paying attention and listening carefully can we discern that he's just playing the part without feeling any connection to it. He may look like a *chacham*, but he's really a *rasha*.

We may find someone who appears to be a *rasha*, shooting barbs and jibes at the religion he's surrounded with. Is he bad? Ask yourself why children tease. "You ca-a-n't catch me, nyah, nyah, nyah kish kish!" Isn't it because they want you to chase after them? If they didn't, they'd be happy you weren't catching them and keep their mouths shut.

By openly taunting you about the customs and rituals we perform, these children, and even adults, are subconsciously begging you to show them the truth and help them believe in what you believe in, and find the beauty, serenity, and security that exist within Judaism.

We are surrounded all the time by people who could, should, and would want to understand more and be more knowledgeable, but are embarrassed to ask for fear of looking foolish. I know I'm one of those. Sometimes, we face our fears and ask. But if we don't, we would welcome and appreciate someone reaching out to us.

If you feel you know everything, or would NOT want someone to share with you or guide you, ask yourself if who you see in the mirror is really who you are. It's a perfect question for Pesach, when we look for questions about redemption.

So let's take some time to put things in order, starting with ourselves. Then we can look around us, and make sure we put the right face on what we see.

Pesach: Being Machmir

*P*ESACH IS THE FESTIVAL of our freedom. It's supposed to be that, actually, though it seems more like when we left the servitude of *Mitzrayim* for the servitude of our kitchens and housecleaning.

This topic has been written about to death, but every year, men and women, or at least, women, make themselves and their families crazy getting ready for Pesach. "Oh no! Purim is next week? That means Pesach cleaning is around the corner! Oh man, that's not fair. How much can one woman/man/child/nuclear physicist attempting to negate *chametz* molecules with WD-40 and a blowtorch do?"

I really wonder if this is what *Chazal* had in mind when they discussed eliminating *chametz*. Of course, in those days it was much easier. You could just wash off the floor (literally), put on a new layer of dirt, and if worse came to worst, just burn down your hut and start again. But not so today. Now we have things like cinder block, linoleum, and arson laws.

But what would they say if they saw the things we do? Well, of course you should vacuum out the back of your closet, isn't that where you eat cookies when you're hiding from your kids? And cleaning between floor tiles with toothpicks is obviously of utmost importance. And who knows how much *chametz* built up in the furnace? But what about some of the *crazy* stuff we do?

I know the prevalent *minhag* is to go a little crazy to avoid *chametz*, and it was in this vein that the custom of not eating *gebrokhts* (basically, no more matzah balls) was established. But, I sometimes wonder how much of what we do borders on *bal tosif* (adding new mitzvos) — a big no-no.

A number of years ago, I was at a supermarket in Baltimore the week before Pesach and a woman was holding her items instead of putting them on the conveyor belt. I moved my groceries to make room for her but she said, "No, thanks, this is my Pesach stuff, I don't want to put it on the *chametzdike* conveyor belt."

Now, at the time, I was learning *Yoreh De'ah* and the *halachos* of such things as mixing meat and milk, and I knew that there was no magical transference of *chametz* possible from the clean and dry conveyor to her closed packages of Pesach socks or whatever she had, so I told her so. "There's really no problem," I told her. "Halachically speaking there's nothing to worry about."

"I know," she replied, "but I'm being *machmir*."

Machmir? *Machmir*?! What does she mean *machmir*? *Machmir* is when something is a *she'eilah*, or even a remote possibility. Not when it's nothing. Jokingly, my father said, "Next year they'll cover the conveyor belt for Pesach." We had a good laugh, but the joke was on us. The next year, they did!

A few weeks ago, just before *Rosh Chodesh* Nisan, I went to my local kosher supermarket and saw that two lanes were covered with contact paper and had special signs designating them for "Passover Use Only." Even with all the other lanes full, and nobody in those lines, people couldn't use the Passover lanes. I couldn't convince the Hispanic cashier to scan my non-*chametz* items and let me wave the *chametz* items over the scanner without touching it, even if I removed it *toch k'dei dibbur*. Well, at least she didn't stop to wonder if my green beans were *kitniyos*.

Perhaps the store had to do it for people like my "*machmir*" friend in Baltimore. I suppose it's mostly harmless, as long as we understand that this craziness is self-imposed and not what the *Ribono shel Olam* demands. I wonder sometimes if He shakes

His head at us and wonders, "That's not MY Torah; what are they thinking?!"

On the other hand, it is well known that many noble Jews have always been more careful regarding Pesach. Many European Jews would not eat dairy the whole Pesach for fear of *chametz*-contaminated milk products. R' Gifter *z"l* once told me the story of when his mother came to visit him and he had gone to a farm to get milk. They had been there as the cows were milked so it was *chalav Yisrael* and there was no worry of *chametz*. But she wouldn't eat it. She said, "*Nein, mein teiyera. Fahr deer iz kosher, fahr meer nisht* (No, my dear. For you it is kosher, but not for me)."

So, next year, when you're chasing your neighbor's cat to clean the crumbs from the bells in his collar, remember that Pesach is really supposed to be a joyous holiday celebrating our Redemption, not a time of reluctant drudgery. Keep in mind that it's about removing the *chametz* from your *neshamah*, and cleaning house internally as a preparation for living a Torah life, the only real way to be free.

And if you see me put my shrink-wrapped box of potato starch on the uncovered conveyor? "*Fahr meer iz kosher, fahr deer nisht* (For me it's kosher, maybe not for you)."

Shavuos: The Ten-Dollar Gym

P EOPLE OFTEN COME UP to me and say, "I've got an article idea for you." Usually it's some pet peeve of theirs which they see as terribly rude, annoying, or wrong. Sometimes, it's something inspirational or special, like when the rain stopped just long enough for *chametz*-burning to go on, and then started again.

This time, someone had a concept and said, "If anyone can come up with a good article about this, it's Jonathan Gewirtz." He had been speaking to the manager of a gym which charges ten dollars a month. "How can you make money on ten dollars a month?" he asked.

"Look around," said the manager. "You see all these people here? These aren't the ones I make money on. I make money on the people who pay ten dollars every month and never show up."

"I don't understand," asked our guest, "Why do they keep paying if they don't come?"

"It's just ten dollars," replied the gym staffer. "They tell themselves, 'I'm not going to cancel. I'm going to start going again next month,' or 'It's almost January (or spring, or summer, or school season). I'll start then and it'll be great.' And so it goes. They let it ride because they plan to come to the gym, but it never happens."

Now, dear readers, I'm not focused on whether or not the gym is making money, or whether you will actually go to a gym if it costs you more money. I'm focused on the idea that keeps people paying month after month.

You see, the people who pay but don't show up are not saying that they don't mind throwing money away. I don't think you'd see any of them take a ten-dollar bill and throw it into the street. People like their money.

Instead, what they're really saying, deep down, is, "It's not too late. I want to stay a member of the gym because I know it's good for me and I should start going more regularly. I can do it."

What an idea! Think about it. Deep down they know what's good and that just because you don't look like a body-builder today is no reason you can't trim a few pounds tomorrow. You don't need to devote major resources to it, just be dedicated and find it important.

If you've ever exercised, especially when you didn't want to, you know how wonderful you feel afterwards. You're glad you pushed yourself. You know it was time well-spent. You feel proud of yourself and rightfully so.

Now, what about if you were exhausted and just wanted to plop down on the couch with a book (or better yet, *without a book!*), but instead you picked up a *sefer*, called a friend who was feeling down, or went out to a *shiur*. You pushed yourself to do what you knew was good for your soul. Afterwards, you probably felt like a million dollars; proud as a peacock.

I've been known to wake up very early in the morning to learn. It's not easy pulling myself out of bed, but I can tell you that when I close the Gemara or finish my weekly *dvar Torah*, I am not thinking about the missing sleep. I'm thinking, "Wow, that was invigorating. I'm so happy I did that. I rock. Go me!"

Shavuos is a time for everyone who has been pushing off their involvement in Torah until they've got more time, or more energy, or less stress, to say, "I want to do this *for me*. I can do it. This is the time I'm going to make it a habit and stick to it."

Because, you know, when you miss it, it's not just ten bucks. It's time. Even if you might throw ten dollars out the window, would you do it to 43,200 minutes each and every month? Think time is money? Forget it. *Money doesn't even come close.*

So resolve to get spiritually healthy, make good choices, and start leading a wholesome Torah lifestyle. Besides, when that's your goal, you can still enjoy your cheesecake on Shavuos without feeling guilty — and more than that, it's a mitzvah!

Three Weeks: I Could Care Less

A S I CLEANED UP my deck, I looked over to the above-ground pool I got for my kids and made a mental note that I had to buy more chlorine. Then I started to think about when they would use it next, and how when it came to the Nine Days I would try to explain to them why I wasn't swimming. "It's because the *Beis HaMikdash* was destroyed and we feel sad, so we don't swim or eat meat."

Now, my five-year-old is smart, but I can't imagine her understanding that. I mean, she can understand that the *Beis HaMikdash* was destroyed, but will it mean anything to her? I remembered what *Chazal* say that each generation understands less about the *Churban* than the previous one.

The Midrash relates that R' Yochanan elucidated sixty interpretations of the verse in *Megillas Eichah*, "*Bila Hashem v'lo chamal* — Hashem consumed and was devoid of compassion," while his teacher R' Yehudah HaNasi only revealed twenty-four. Was R' Yochanan a greater *talmid chacham* than his teacher? No. What happened was that after R' Yehudah HaNasi expounded twenty-four meanings of the verse he broke down in uncontrollable tears and was unable to continue. He didn't even live at the time of the *Churban*, yet he was so distraught. His disciple, however, was a generation removed and did not feel the same level of anguish.

I thought about that. My children will not feel the loss of the *Beis HaMikdash* as much as I do. It will mean less to them. Then a scary, scary thought crossed my mind — Is that even possible?!

Is it possible for my children to care less about the *Beis Ha-Mikdash* than I do? Do I really have any deep emotion about it or am I just going through the motions of the Nine Days because that's the thing to do? What kind of connection and loss do I feel for the home of the Almighty? To think that I am so far removed that I might question if there was a further disconnect was frightening indeed.

In *Shulchan Aruch, Hanhagos ha'adam baboker* (1:3), the *Mechaber* says, "It is proper for every Heaven-fearing person to be distressed and concerned over the destruction of the *Beis HaMikdash*." It is not just a nice thing; it is a *halachah*! Yet do we do this? Are we concerned about the *Beis HaMikdash*?

My wife and I were just discussing the Nine Days and the common practice in camps to have a *siyum* made on a *masechta* of Gemara so they can eat *fleishig* meals. Often, campers may not even realize that it's the Nine Days because every night they are eating meat. One camp I know used to have three or four *siyumim* during the Nine Days, but because they wanted to impress upon the children that there is a period of mourning going on, they decided to limit it to one or two.

The question for us is: could we care less? Do we have a connection to the *Churban*, the loss of the *Beis HaMikdash* which was the starting point of all light and *berachah* in the world through which Hashem conducted His blessing and power? If we don't have a connection, is there anything we can do?

The answer is yes, we have a connection, and yes, we can strengthen it. We have a connection because each Jew feels the loss in his heart, no matter how faintly. This holy spark realizes it's missing the fuel of the manifest presence of *HaKadosh Baruch Hu* on earth.

Now how to strengthen it? Simple. We must reflect on the troubles surrounding us, and realize that just as the *Beis HaMikdash* was the source of all *berachah*, so is the lack of the *Beis HaMikdash* the source of all suffering and pain. Every rocket fired on an innocent home, every young child who dies suddenly, every family left without a father or mother and every person maimed in accidents all link back to the vacuum left when the *Beis HaMikdash* was taken away from us.

We can learn about the *Churban*, the *midrashim*, the stories. We can study the Holocaust, a *churban* of unbelievable proportions which only happened a generation or two ago, and realize that Hashem is talking to us, wistfully wishing Himself for the *Beis HaMikdash* to be rebuilt.

In *Shemoneh Esreh*, we pray for the flourishing of the salvation of our people through the descendant of David HaMelech, Mashiach. We say, "*Ki l'yishuas'cha kivinu kol hayom* — For Your salvation we hope each day." In *Nusach Sefard*, many *siddurim* have the words "*u'mitzapim l'yishua* — and we hope for salvation" written in parentheses at the end of that phrase. Many say these words, but it is said that these words were not part of the prayer, but a "stage instruction" as it were, to the *mispallel*.

When you say these words, that you wait for Hashem's salvation each day, do you mean it? Do you really look for Hashem's return to us? Therefore, there is a reminder, "Hope for Salvation!" At this point in the *davening*, focus on what that means and truly yearn for it. It is possible to strengthen our connection and deepen our understanding of the *Churban*, but we must make a conscious effort to do so.

To that end, I have a challenge for all of my dear readers. The *Mishnah Berurah* on the above-mentioned *halachah* regarding being distressed over the destruction of the *Beis HaMikdash* quotes the Shelah that one should recite *Al Naharos Bavel* (Psalm 137) before *bentshing* during the week and *Shir HaMaalos* (Psalm 26) on Shabbos. We all say *Shir HaMaalos* before *bentshing* on Shabbos, but how many of us say *Al Naharos Bavel* before *bentshing* during the week?

The challenge is this: During the Nine Days, make sure that you wash and eat bread at several weekday meals. When it comes time to *bentsch,* say *Al Naharos Bavel* and think about what you're saying. Concentrate on the meaning (look it up if you need to). See if you can feel disconnected and distant from the *Churban.* See if you can help being drawn to tears as you read the words of David HaMelech, the king who captured the emotions of our nation in his songs.

I bet you care more than you realize.

Tisha B'Av: A Time to Build

I REMEMBER A STORY I heard from R' Paysach Krohn about a fellow who was having his house painted. He explained to the Irish painter that he wanted a large square left unpainted, near the door. The painter didn't understand. "Why would you want to ruin a beautiful paint job by leaving a part unfinished?" he asked incredulously.

"It's because our Temple was destroyed," replied the Jew.

"Oh, I'm sorry to hear that," said the subdued painter. "I didn't hear about that, was it nearby?"

"No," said the homeowner, "it was in Jerusalem."

"Ah," replied the painter, "the holy city. I don't keep up with the news from Israel. When did it happen?"

"About two thousand years ago," answered our friend.

At this point, the painter threw his hands up and said, "Two thousand years ago? Come on, why can't you let bygones be bygones?!"

If we were only talking about a building which lost its meaning many years ago, like the Coliseum or the Parthenon, maybe we could, but not our *Beis HaMikdash*.

Often during the Three Weeks, I have been questioned by non-Jews about my beard becoming unruly, or not shaving the rest of my face. (For those who thought I was *Chassidish, oops!* The cat is out of the bag.) Being that we are not allowed to teach Torah to a non-Jew, my answer had to make sense without going too in-depth.

I would tell people that it was a period of mourning because the Temple was destroyed. Some have asked the "bygones" question, but generally people are respectful when you speak about religious convictions. (Note: You have to be respectful of Judaism as well, if you want others to respect you for practicing your religion — i.e., that if it means something to you, not that you're just going through the motions, you will earn respect for it.)

When I thought more about it, I realized that we're not mourning the fact that the *Beis HaMikdash* was destroyed; we're mourning the fact that it hasn't been rebuilt!

That's a key distinction that I think is all too often lost on us. We talk about the *Churban* as something that happened to someone else, to another time, to another generation. That's why we don't feel connected to it. But look around. We're experiencing *Churban* in an ongoing fashion.

The *Beis HaMikdash* represented a relationship with our Heavenly Father. Today, more than ever, people, even those who are *shomrei Torah u'mitzvos*, feel disenfranchised. They don't feel that special bond to Hashem and because of that they can't find true happiness. People look for happiness in physical indulgences because they don't find fulfillment in spiritual ones. That's not a failing of the religion, it's a result of the *Churban*, and it continues to wreak havoc on our people and cause destruction.

Chazal tell us that any generation in which the *Beis HaMikdash* is not built is as if it was destroyed. We frequently look back at the previous generations and put the onus on them. If *they* would have had *ahavas chinam*, if *they* hadn't been involved in promiscuous activity, if *they* hadn't put other things (such as money and power) ahead of Hashem on their priorities, then *we* would have a *Beis HaMikdash*.

Herbert Hoover said that old men declare war but it is the youth who must fight and die. We have the opposite approach to building the *Beis HaMikdash*. We think it's the job of the older generations, the *tzaddikim* and *rabbanim* and righteous women to bring *Mashiach*. As R' Gifter *z"l* would say, "BUNK!! It's *our* responsibility." And we've already seen it.

Rachmana Litzlan, young people are dying suddenly and we shake our heads and say, "What a tragedy." Well it's time to stop shaking our heads and start doing something about it. Yes, there is a time to weep, but now it is the time to build.

I heard that one segment of *Klal Yisrael* called upon its members to be more careful in *tznius*, and to bring in Shabbos a few minutes earlier. Shabbos is the sign of the bond between us and Hashem, so it makes sense that to enhance that and recognize its significance would be a step in the right direction. *Tznius*, too, is a prerequisite for *berachah*. The second *luchos*, given to Moshe Rabbeinu in privacy, were the ones which lasted. *Tznius* means we don't brag about what we have, or we might lose it. We don't use our mouths for foul speech or off-color comments because they are what separate us from the animals, and make us closer to God.

This is one response, but I'm sure there are others. All of us can find things in our day, stray mitzvos without a home, opportunities to do a kindness, to improve ourselves spiritually, to do something to add just one more brick to the third *Beis HaMikdash*.

Pinchas was one man alone, but he did what he could, and was rewarded with the *kehunah*. How appropriate then, as we know that Pinchas is Eliyahu, that it is he who will come, speedily and in our days, to herald the arrival of *Mashiach* as a result of all our individual efforts.

During the period of the Three Weeks, we shouldn't focus on the fact that the *Beis HaMikdash* was destroyed. That may be too difficult, too foreign. Instead, we should focus on the fact that it hasn't yet been rebuilt, and do what we can to change that.

Elul: Preparing for the Days of AAUUGGHH!!

*I*N MY YESHIVAH, TELZ in Cleveland, Ohio, Elul was a magical time. It conveyed special meaning and feeling as we strove to improve ourselves in preparation for Rosh Hashanah and Yom Kippur.

There were special *shmuessen* (ethical lectures) designed to inspire us, we learned *Mussar* out loud as a group, and in general, the mood was somber and more solemn than other times of the year.

In fact, there was an old joke about a car driving through Yerushalayim on Shabbos. The Yerushalmi screamed, "Shabbos! Shabbos!" The Telzer yelled, "Elul! Elul!" [Ed. Note: *The irony being that Shabbos wasn't sufficient to inspire righteous indignation.*]

One day in late Elul, I was looking at my trusty Ezras Torah *luach*, reading what we would be doing in the coming weeks. I read how on *erev Rosh Hashanah* we get up before *alos hashachar* (waaayyy before humans were meant to get up) to say extended *Selichos* (you mean there's more?!), plus that it is customary to fast half a day on *erev Rosh Hashanah*.

My thoughts spiraled out of control as I conjured up visions of dark mornings, long dreary *Selichos*, and constant sleep deprivation (and that was even *before* having kids). Though I'm ashamed to admit it, I thought to myself, "I can't wait for MarCheshvan!"

Okay, that all took place in about three nanoseconds, and then

I caught myself. I imagine I'm not the only one who's ever had those thoughts but I hope I'm also not the only one who did a retraction instantaneously.

If you look at *Selichos* and getting up early as *avodah* (work), then it may very well seem dreary. But I have another way to look at it, as I will now explain.

I've invented a hypothetical contest. In it, someone gets the opportunity to work for Ronald Grump, wealthy real estate mogul, toupee model and entrepreneur (any similarity to real persons is purely coincidental). There's a catch. He doesn't want to just tell you what to do; he wants to see how you think. He will give you six weeks to pitch him your best ideas and why you're the one he should entrust to run the projects.

It gets better. Mr. Grump ("The Ronald," as he likes to call himself) has very specific times when he wants to hear what you have to say. He wants you to meet him for breakfast. Did I mention he eats breakfast on the subway at 4 A.M.?

You've been chosen as a contestant. What do you do? If he likes your style, your starting salary would shadow that of members of Congress... ALL OF THEM PUT TOGETHER.

Instead, you decide that it's too much trouble and stick to your current lifestyle. Thanks anyway, Mr. Grump — but I'M TIRED!

Okay, so that's not likely. We all know we'd be there at 3:45 with coffee and Danish and a big can of Lysol. It's not often you get an opportunity like that so you'd be crazy to miss it.

Well, each year, we get the same opportunity. Actually, it's a much better one. When we get up early for *Selichos*, we're meeting with THE BOSS. We may be crowded into a shul, but His attention is focused on US. He's ready to listen to our ideas. When we blow the *shofar* and say *L'David Hashem Ori*, we're telling Him our gameplan for success, and it's all built around Him.

If He likes what we have to say, and feels we're sincere, we'll get a successful year of life, health, wealth, happiness, and all the good that comes with being God's right-hand man, His "apprentice" if you will — doing His business and making Him [and ourselves] happy.

In the *Haftorah* read on fast days, the *Navi* Yeshayahu (55:6) tells us, "Seek out Hashem while He can be found; call to Him while He is close." The six weeks from the beginning of Elul are when He is closest and ready for us to pitch Him our ideas of why we deserve this chance. Who could pass that up?

Oh, and did I mention the best part of the contest? We're not competing against anyone — but ourselves.

Rosh Hashanah: Signs

*A*S THE DEADLINE FOR my next article loomed closer, I drew a blank. I had no idea what to write about. Images of lonely writers with mental block assailed me. Typewriters sitting in garbage cans (for those of you who don't know what I mean, you must be too young — imagine the guy throwing his monitor out the window instead), crumpled sheets of paper, depressing tales of writers who never made it.

"Please Hashem," I thought, "Give me a sign." Wait a minute, signs! Perfect, that's what I'll write about! You see, the article would be out just before Rosh Hashanah and that is the perfect time to talk about signs, omens, and symbolism.

Almost every Jew knows that we dip an apple in honey so that we should have a sweet new year; even the non-Jews know it, thanks to Sue Bee and her friends at the honey factory. But those of us who are more familiar with Jewish traditions know that this is just the tip of the iceberg (which, by the way, is a *siman* done by eating just the very smallest edge of your lettuce leaf, but I digress…)

On Rosh Hashanah, we make all kinds of symbolic acts, usually involving food. That, more than anything, probably proves the authentic Jewish origins of this custom. The common symbols we eat are listed in the *machzor* and include: the head of a lamb or fish so we should be, "the head and not the tail"; pomegranates, so we should be "as full of mitzvos as a pomegranate"; and carrots. Why carrots? Because in Yiddish the word for carrots is "*merren*" which can also mean "more." We appreciate what we have, but we want "more" *zechusim*, "more" *chesed*, "more" of everything.

People have taken this to new levels. One prominent Rav was known to eat peas on Rosh Hashanah to have "peace on earth." You could eat lettuce, half a raisin and celery so Hashem might "Lettuce half a raisin celery" (Let us have a raise in salary), or put a cabbage in your briefcase to get "a head at the office."

What we see is that even though these foods have no special significance other than their chance homophonic similarities to something, they are respected as *siman* food. Doesn't seem too magical, does it? So how does it work?

The thing to understand is that *simanim*, the signs we assemble on Rosh Hashanah, don't work by magic. One origin of this custom is the Gemara in *Horayos* 12a which says that one should be accustomed to view various items at the beginning of the year. That's good news for those squeamish among us who can't quite stomach the idea of eating something like a lamb's head that can watch us as we do. We don't need to eat it, just look at it. Okay, so we know where it comes from, but do we know how it works?

The Gemara just before the one mentioned above says that if a person wants to see if he will live out the year he should light a candle in a wind-proof room during the *Aseres Yemei Teshuvah*. If it stays lit, he knows he will live out the year. But what if it goes out? The Gemara doesn't say. The Maharsha says, "If it goes out, it doesn't mean anything."

You see, *simanim* and signs can only be for good. If a person sees what he considers a "bad omen" and then something bad happens, it's because in his fear and trepidation about the bad sign he has somehow negatively affected his *mazel* and that's what caused the trouble.

This knowledge is of great use! That means that if you see something as a good sign, your happiness improves your *mazel*, leading to good things, too. I'm reminded of the story about a multi-millionaire who used to stop and pick up pennies on the street. Someone asked him why he needed the penny. Showing him the letters on the small coin, the rich man said, "You see what it says here? It says 'In God We Trust.' I know it isn't me who made all this money, it was God's benevolent hand. Whenever I see a penny, I just know He put it there to send me a message and remind me that He's watching out for me. Isn't that worth picking up?"

By taking even the smallest occurrence as a good sign, we can ensure that good things happen. And if we think something is a bad sign? Remember, "It doesn't mean anything!"

Aseres Yemei Teshuvah:
You're Stronger Than You Think
Divrei Chizuk for the Yamim Nora'im

A FEW WEEKS AGO, THERE was something in the house that I didn't want to eat. Let me rephrase that — I *wanted* to eat it, but I knew that I shouldn't. I don't remember if it was ice cream or macaroni and cheese or something along those lines that I really didn't need. I was fighting my urges, then told myself, "I'm going to eat something *fleishig* (meat, as opposed to dairy or pareve) so I can't have it." Then it hit me.

What difference would it make if I was *fleishig*? Who was stopping me? — ME! If I could stop myself from eating it because I was *fleishig*, why couldn't I stop myself without eating the meat? I think I passed it up that night, but that's not the point because I'd had a revelation.

What remained with me was the fact that I was able to be in control of myself when I didn't feel there was an alternative, when I had no choice. Let's take another example. On Rosh Hashanah, we know (most of us do, at least) that one may not speak from the time the *berachah* is said on the *shofar* until after the hundredth blast. If we speak, we have not fulfilled the proper mitzvah of *tekias shofar*.

Somehow, tens of thousands of us survive without talking during Rosh Hashanah *davening* for several long hours. So why is it that we can't do that on a regular Shabbos? Or a weekday *Shacharis*? People speak, joke, comment, and *kibbitz* when they're supposed to be conversing with Hashem — you know, the One who gives us EVERYTHING — like the things we're *davening* for!

What about when one of the days of Rosh Hashanah falls on Shabbos? When it falls on a weekday, people refrain from speaking for fear of breaking the connection of the *berachah* and the blowing of the *shofar*. What about when there's no *shofar* because it's Shabbos? Do they think, "Whew, I can do what I want because there's no *shofar*?"

A friend mentioned to me tonight that the Manchester Rosh Yeshivah *z"l* used to say, "People don't talk by *shofar* because from a young age it was ingrained in them that they could not speak. Could you imagine if we did the same thing with *lashon hara*?" The same way one who inadvertently spoke out before all one hundred blasts of the *shofar* were complete would hit himself in the head and feel like a fool, that's how it should be if one slips and says something derogatory about another Jew (yes, even if it's true!). He should be kicking himself for even thinking that way.

During the *Aseres Yemei Teshuvah*, the *Shulchan Aruch* says, people are more stringent about bread baked by a non-Jew. Why are we stricter during this time period? Are we trying to fool God?

On the contrary — we're trying to show the truth to mankind. When we maintain higher levels of behavior between Rosh Hashanah and Yom Kippur, it does more than just provide the benefit of starting off on a higher level. (Think of a sled or bicycle going down a hill. The higher the start, the further the rider will go.)

What it also shows us is how we are capable of doing these things all the time, if we realized that we could do it. Imagine for a moment we thought about things we manage to do once in a while, which could be done all the time.

We've already had our first example in the "speaking in shul" category. We saw that we are able to refrain from talking to anyone else but Hashem in shul on Rosh Hashanah. That means we could and should do it all the time.

What about not speaking ill of someone else? Imagine you were talking to someone's father or mother and their child had done something bad. Would you share the "juicy" gossip with them? Clearly not. They would not be amused. For those of you who think that you would still say it, let's make it easier. That person is your boss, the one who will decide whether you get your raise or whether you will have a job next month. Do you still have the urge to smear his child's reputation, or do you maybe decide to hold your tongue? I'm guessing you don't say anything. You obviously have the capacity and ability to refrain from speaking about others, so the problem isn't "I can't," it's "I don't want to."

One of my pet peeves (besides the shopping carts, which I continue to remove from parking spaces, especially in the rain) is people taking off their *tallis* and *tefillin* early in shul. Why do you need to take them off before *davening* is over? If you were making a *bris* in the shul you'd find a way to keep them on.

So, maybe you have to go to work. But why are you standing and schmoozing afterwards? And what if you were told you had to keep a cast on a broken arm for six weeks? Would you take it off after four because you were in a rush? It's not different. One is for your physical health and one is for your spiritual health. And what's the excuse of the fellow who's retired, yet he does it too? Or the boy in school whose *tefillin* are wrapped before he says the *Shir shel Yom*? It doesn't have to be this way; you CAN do it!

Couldn't control yourself from yelling at the idiot who...? What about if he was about to give you a hot stock tip or pay you for a job you did? How many times has a customer dropped something in a retail store and we say, "It's ok," because we expect to keep making money on the future sales? That means we can control ourselves if we recognize the stakes.

So next time Rosh Hashanah falls on Shabbos, remember that

if there would have been a *shofar* blowing, you would have been able to keep yourself from talking, and do it even when there isn't.

When you sit down at the meal, treat your family as if they were prized customers, at whom you'd never get upset or annoyed. When you wish people a sweet new year, really mean it, as you could if you were wishing goodness on your own child.

As you go on through the year, and you find things difficult, imagine a scenario when you'd be able to overcome your urges, and you'll soon find yourself overcoming them in all situations.

Then, when Rosh Hashanah rolls around next year, you will be able to humbly say, "I guess I didn't know my own strength."

Yom Kippur: Getting the Message

O NE YOM KIPPUR, SOMEONE had brought a baby to shul for *Minchah/Ne'ilah* and the infant was crying incessantly. My initial response was, "Why can't they get that kid out of here or at least keep him quiet? Don't they realize they're disturbing people?" (See *Mishnah Berurah* 98:3 for more on the subject.)

That was my initial response. However, my second response, an instant later, was to get an inspiring message for myself as I approached *Ne'ilah*. Just before *Chazaras HaShat"z* I whispered to the *chazan*, "Remember this while you're *davening*: First of all, the baby is crying, saying, 'Daddy, pick me up and hold me close.' Second, it won't stop crying until it gets what it wants." That's what we should be doing on Yom Kippur — asking our Father to bring us close.

I thought it was a fabulous message, and it inspired me in my *davening*. Had I given in to the cynicism, I probably would have thought some things about the parents that I would have had to ask *mechilah* for. Instead, I "got the message," and heard God's voice calling out to me loud and clear.

Often, I think Hashem communicates with us but because of the subtle nature of these messages we miss them. Other times, we miscategorize the messages and don't realize where they're coming from. People tell us things and we don't recognize the original Source.

Sometimes, people insult us. We get offended and say, "I didn't deserve that!" We may have a point that the other person should have spoken more considerately, but ultimately, if we heard it, it's because Hashem wanted us to. Saying, "I didn't deserve that" is a very arrogant thing to do, as if we are perfect and know what we deserve. When we remember that Hashem is the Master Puppeteer, guiding all the occurrences in our lives, we might recognize that He's telling us we *did* deserve it.

When people "push our buttons" (and this includes spouses and children — *especially* children), we should listen closely. Perhaps then we will hear *HaKadosh Baruch Hu* saying to the *malachim*, "Hmmm, let's test this one. I wonder if he is worthy of winning the lottery." If we succeed in controlling ourselves, we not only gain stature in the eyes of the other person and can almost physically feels our souls expanding, but we also prove ourselves more loyal servants of God and worthy of His blessing.

Then there are other times, like when we overhear conversations. We should look at those instances to see if there's a message for us. Just as one who gets an *aliyah* should look at the *parshah* he is given and seek out a message, these snippets of conversation are intended for us. If we heard them, there's a reason.

While writing this article, I had a doctor's appointment. The doctor prescribed some medicine and I asked if they had any samples to get me started until I got the prescription filled. He said he didn't think they did. I said to him, "Actually, you do have samples. I am in the midst of writing an article about getting the message, and one thing I wrote this morning was about overheard conversations. About two minutes ago, I just heard one of your nurses ask another if they could give a patient samples of that very drug." I got the samples, but even more exciting was the fact that God Himself had sent me a message and I got it. I realized that I heard that conversation so I would know something I otherwise had no way of knowing.

Sometimes, the message may even be in words spoken to us. Then we have to look beneath the surface of the conversation to find the subliminal messages from Above.

For those readers who are not familiar with professional baseball, it's basically a bunch of men standing out in a field swatting flies and getting paid millions of dollars to refuse to sign autographs for little children.

Recently, the New York Mets were in a playoff series to determine whether they would go to the World Series. They made it to the seventh and deciding game. At the bottom of the ninth inning, with two outs and bases loaded, Carlos Beltran came up to bat. He was struck out and the third strike came as he stood there with the bat on his shoulder. (If you really didn't know what baseball was, by now you must be thoroughly confused. Keep reading, maybe it will make some sense.)

After that third strike, the game was over. There were no more chances to score runs, no more chances to advance to the World Series, nothing. There was just silence and a lot of tears.

R' Ephraim Wachsman *shlit"a* once used a baseball analogy to explain the concept of *tzipisa l'Yeshuah*, (waiting for *Mashiach* and Redemption). He said, "When the coach tells the batter, 'It's the bottom of the ninth, and there are two outs,' what is he telling him? That he'll be able to take his tight shoes off soon? Not at all! He's telling him that now is the time to buckle down and perform."

Similarly, when we await *Mashiach*'s arrival, it must be with the understanding that when *Mashiach* comes, there will be no more *yetzer hara*, and therefore no more chances to score points (redeemable for Heavenly rewards, see full Terms and Conditions for details) or for advancement. We need to realize that now is the time to buckle down because later there may be only silence and tears over the lost opportunities.

This message is powerful by itself, but was strengthened by

something my *chavrusa* said to me. "I'm not a big Mets fan, but what upset me is that Beltran went down without swinging! I hate when that happens. It's the bottom of the ninth, two outs and bases loaded. Swing for goodness sake!"

I know that he spoke a deeper message. We may think that with the arrival of *Mushiach*, the actions of the *tzaddikim* are what will count. But in truth, every one of us is standing at that plate, with the whole game riding on our next action. It's true; we might strike out. But, at least, we have to go down swinging.

Sukkos: Turning Over an Old Leaf

O NE OF THE BENEFITS of living in the suburbs is the ability to witness the wonders of nature as the leaves turn colors each autumn. Driving down the Palisades Parkway is like driving through a tunnel of reds and golds. Looking to the mountains, I see the luxurious blanket of fall colors adorning the horizon.

As I left shul one morning, and caught a glimpse of the blazing color glinting in the early morning sun, I paused to thank Hashem for the beauty of the natural world around us, and for the opportunity to enjoy this majestic show. My mother a"h always loved the fall foliage and maybe I have her to thank for some of my appreciation thereof.

But then I began thinking of something else I had heard about leaves. I don't recall which lecturer it was who spoke about the topic but he mentioned something that should give us pause. When we see the colors in the leaves, it's not because they are growing and gaining strength. On the contrary, they're breaking down and dying!

Photosynthesis halts as the shorter days no longer provide the necessary sunlight for the process of breaking down carbon dioxide into oxygen and glucose. The green chlorophyll begins to disappear and the colors emerge — not due to beautiful growth, but due to inevitable death.

Now, this sounds depressing, but when you know how to look at it, it really isn't. We can learn a valuable lesson from the leaves and when we do, we will be able to enjoy the beauty that much more.

R' Avigdor Miller *z"l* famously spoke about the brilliant color in an orange which makes us want to eat it. "But," he says, "look inside, and it's white. Why? Because the Master of the World won't waste color where it won't be seen and is unnecessary." If that's so, the message of the autumn leaves must be very important to be put all over the world where the dramatic color it provides is admired by millions. So what is the message?

It's interesting to note that many of the fruits and vegetables associated with autumn share those orange, gold, and deep purple colors which make the leaves so striking. Squash, pumpkins and gourds make us think of fall, giving thanks, and the approaching cooler weather. Autumn is the time of harvest, when we gather in the fruits of our labors all summer and enjoy what we've prepared as we approach the long winter ahead.

That's exactly what the leaves are doing, utilizing whatever they've created while the long sunny days made it possible for them to be productive, and waiting for the opportunity once again to begin growing leaves and starting the cycle of being productive again.

Sukkos comes at this time of the year and we focus on our joy. But if we think about it, all the produce that was growing until now is picked — plucked from its source of life — and now sits, dead, in our storerooms and pantries. Should we truly rejoice over these once-thriving life forms which no longer have the chance to grow?

Of course the question is preposterous, since the whole purpose of planting food is to have it grow and provide sustenance for us once it is harvested. Even animals, which are raised for food, fulfill their purpose for being only when they are turned into nutritious victuals that provide a source of life for growing boys and girls. The joy we experience at the ingathering comes not from the death of the plant or animal, but from the realization that we have achieved what we set out to do.

When we see the leaves changing colors, it is a sign that their work is complete. They have diligently turned an unbreathable gas, carbon dioxide, into fresh oxygen for humankind and animals alike. They have stored up enough food for their respective trees to provide sustenance through the winter ahead. At this time, they have reason to celebrate their success with a show of stunning color. But there's more.

If we reflect on what happens to the leaves, we see a parallel in mankind. The Torah commands us, "*Mipnei seivah takum v'hadarta p'nei zakein* — And you shall honor the presence of an elder, and you shall rise in the presence of an old person." The Torah praises old age and calls it worthy of respect and honor. While the non-Torah world praises youth and beauty, we see the wisdom of life experience as a glowing crown upon those who have trod upon this earth for seventy years or more.

This is similar to the leaves which, as they approach the end of their lives, exhibit a fiery presence which makes us take note. So many of our greatest people became more well-known as they approached the end of their lives. These *gedolim* flourish as they approach their final years, much as the leaves do. So what is the lesson that is so important to all of us?

I would like to suggest that the common thread between the leaves, the harvested produce, and the elders, is a reduced connection to the earthly plane. As the photosynthesis ceases, the green chlorophyll ebbs away to reveal the beautiful hues that were really there *the whole time*. The natural process of work production was hiding the inherent beauty of the leaf.

So, too, the day-to-day matters of living tend to mask the greatness inside each of us. Especially for us in America, the concept of everything holy being hidden by "the green" is quite under-standable. However, as we age, we tend to become more detached from running after the dollar, less likely to chase excitement and avenues of pleasure or entertainment. We begin to introspect and find the beauty within ourselves, and seek the connection to a higher power. That wisdom, the life-experience which helps us recognize what's truly important and valuable, is what Judaism finds so praiseworthy.

When we see an elder, we know they have spent their lives preparing for the winter ahead, when they will no longer be able to gather mitzvos and turn moments of life into fuel for *Olam HaBa*. The more they have done their job, the more glorious the showing. We are meant to reflect on this all our years, and Hashem gives us a stark reminder every autumn.

The *Mabul* began and ended in Cheshvan, which is usually the peak month for fall foliage color in much of the world. Not coincidentally, one of the promises Hashem made after the flood was that the seasons would never be suspended. Rather, we would always see the cycle of birth, prodigious growth, glorious ending, and the deathly quiet of winter.

This is to remind us why we are here, and how we can turn the days of our lives into sustenance for our future life in *Olam HaBa* — the life which is our primary existence, but for which one must prepare now. Each year, the autumn leaves flash and gleam this message to us as they repose in splendid color, catching our eyes, and hopefully, our thoughts as well.

Chanukah:
It's All about the Gifts

T HERE I WAS, the night before Chanukah, standing in the kitchen at 4 A.M. in my pajamas, making *cholent* after my daughter commandeered my bed, and my mind started to wander as it is wont to do.

That night, I had received a funeral and *shivah* notice upon the passing of a friend's mother. I got to thinking, as I will sometimes, and wondered what would be said at my own *levayah*. Now, before you go thinking I'm getting all morbid, the fact is that one of the best ways to lead a productive life is to think about what people will say for your *hesped* (eulogy) and make sure they're not left grasping for material.

I'm reminded of the time when one of the janitors in my ye-shivah died. The person in charge of campus personnel, Rabbi W., went to the funeral and, to his shock, was called upon to eulogize the fellow. Well, you can't say someone was a lazy son-of-a-gun with a bad attitude, so he stood there a moment and thought. Then he said, "He lived a good life. He enjoyed good cigars, he enjoyed good whiskey. He knew how to enjoy life." The message was appropriate for an audience like that and the crowd approved, but God help us if someone had to say that about any one of us, *chas v'shalom*.

I started to think about what people might say if I wrote my own *hesped* while I was alive, to be delivered when I was only there in spirit. The listeners would undoubtedly think it made sense, since I am known as a writer. I mean, that's what I do with my life, right? I write articles, I write a weekly *dvar Torah* called the Migdal Ohr...

[We pause now for station identification: *If you do not already receive the Migdal Ohr, send an e-mail with the subject "Subscribe" to info@jewishspeechwriter.com. Enjoy this one-page, English dvar Torah and print some copies for your shul. You'll be glad you did.* Now back to our regularly scheduled article, already in progress...]

...which *Baruch Hashem* reaches people all over the world. I have written letters and brochures for yeshivos, *mosdos*, shuls, etc. I've written poetry, I've written prose. I've written humor, and I write speeches that people feel proud delivering and that the audience enjoys listening to. Once, I was in a printer's shop and I heard someone debating with the printer about the punctuation of a certain sign he wanted to print for his yeshivah dinner. I stopped, walked over, introduced myself as an expert, and helped him reword and edit the sign into a masterpiece.

The question is: Why do I write? Do I do it for the glory? The fame? The big bucks? (as if.)

The answer is quite simple. I write because I can. The *Ribono shel Olam* gave me a talent to write. I didn't study it; I didn't take long hours of classes to learn how to write; I just write. Now, saying I am a good writer is no more arrogant than a professional basketball player saying that he's seven feet tall. It's not arrogance; it's a statement of fact. God made him tall; He made me a writer.

However, when you're given a gift (here's the Chanukah tie-in...) you have an obligation to use it. The basketball player is tall, but unless he practices and uses his height as an advantage in the game, the gift is meaningless.

I can write, but unless I put my talents to good use, using them for *kavod Shamayim*, it's a waste. That's why I write. I write to inspire; I write to make people think; I write to bring people closer to themselves and to Hashem.

When people tell me they love reading my work, I feel fantastic. Not because I am impressed with myself, but because it means I am accomplishing my goal of touching others through my words.

Chanukah is a time for *hallel v'hodaah* (praise and acknowledgment [of what Hashem has done for us]), and it is a time when we celebrate the rededication of the *Beis HaMikdash*.

If I could challenge my readers, I would ask this: This Chanukah, take a good long look at yourself. Recognize the talents and abilities God has blessed you with and find a way to dedicate yourself and those abilities to a good purpose. Don't waste the gifts you've received.

And getting back to my own *hesped*, if I could indeed write my own last line, I think I would be happy if people could honestly say, "He used his gifts to serve Hashem."

Instruction Manual for Life

FOR YEARS, TIME TRAVEL has been a staple of fantasy literature. People have always wanted to be able to move into the future, back to the past, and generally come and go as they please.

Well, unfortunately, that isn't entirely possible yet, but we do participate in time travel on a regular basis. Each day, we are moving forward into the future.

We are faced with decisions, forks in the road, and ponderances about how today's actions will affect the future. How can we know what the right thing to do really is?

Well, before time was created, the Torah existed. In fact, the world, and the time incorporated into it, was based on this blueprint of Torah.

That means that if we want to know how to make our way through planet Earth safely in body, mind, and soul, we should use the Torah as our guidebook, each and every day.

Self-Help (Is) for Dummies

*I*F YOU GO TO a bookstore, you will likely see a huge section entitled "Self-Help Books." The idea being, of course, that the books tell you step by step what you need to do in order to perform the given task. It doesn't matter that they told you exactly what to do — as long as they're not standing right in front of you, then you did it on your own. The question I have is: "Why is it so important for people to do things alone?"

Simply stated, I guess it's a self-esteem issue. We want to be able to say, "Look what I did! I'm good enough, I'm smart enough, and by golly, I can create success for myself." If we would need the help of others, we might feel it diminishes the luster of our own inherent abilities. Often times, this leads to a somewhat less successful outcome than if we had gotten that help.

How many times have we seen a toddler who insists, "I do it!" and then the results are, well, less than desirable? You end up with spilled liquids, mismatched clothing, or a big bill from the plumber or dry cleaner. Had the child been willing to listen to direction, he still could have done the act, but could have avoided some of the problems and failures the adult wanted to prevent by virtue of his own knowledge and experience.

There's an old joke about a very successful fellow in his sixties who was approached by an excited young entrepreneur. "Is it true you're a self-made man?" the youngster asked breathlessly.

"Yes," replied the older man, "and if I had it to do over again, I'd have asked for help."

Wisdom and maturity teach us that not only is it okay to ask for guidance and direction, it actually shows that we're smart enough and secure enough in our identities to do so.

I remember a comic book character named Captain Marvel. In real life he was an awkward young boy, but when he said a special word, he was transformed into a superhero — all grown up, powerful, and able to help others in trouble. Now, comic book superheroes have always had their own stories as to how they got their powers, whether by being bitten by a radioactive spider, from shaking hands with an electric eel, or going up in space in a hot air balloon made of cheddar cheese. It's all nonsense, but Captain Marvel's had something different about it.

Yes, there's no such thing as a magic word that can transform us into something we're not, but here was his word: "SHAZAM!" According to the writers, it was an acronym which stood for six mythical figures (well, one real and five mythical) and when he spoke that word, he was imbued with the wisdom of Solomon, the strength of Hercules (or for our Jewish friends, SHimshon) and so on.

In essence, these comic-book folk were subliminally teaching kids that the way to be a real hero is to take the best of what's out there. Learn from whomever you can, and utilize their knowledge to reach your goals. That is how you grow up to be someone great.

It is well-known that R' Elchonon Wasserman *Hy"d*, as an older student in the Telzer Yeshivah, would ask a boy in *machlakah alef* (about bar-mitzvah age) to review the Gemara with him. This way, R' Elchonon felt he could gain pure, unadulterated *peshat*, the simple meaning of the Gemara's words without the distraction of any *chiddushim* or *pilpul*. The elaborations would come later, but he wanted to get the basics and chose the most appropriate teacher for that skill.

Why wasn't he embarrassed to ask for help, especially from someone clearly much less educated than himself? R' Elchonon understood that when you are looking for success, there's no shame in benefiting from the knowledge of anyone. On the contrary, it's a shame if you don't.

Say you run a business and someone offers you advice. You could say, "He doesn't know this business or how it works, so what he has to say is of no benefit." Of course, that idea might just have been the one to set you on course to greater success than you ever imagined. That's why companies spend millions on consumer research, asking people their opinions even if they have no idea how to run that business.

One company actually started a website allowing people to submit their ideas and discuss and vote on the ideas posted. Then, they took the best ones and put them into practice. They could have said, "We have marketing experts and intelligent people, we don't need your input," but they understood that everyone has something to offer and the smartest people are the ones who listen to everyone. You don't have to necessarily follow their advice, but if you do, then it's you, not they, who deserve credit.

The Torah is based on a *mesorah* (tradition). Those who have gone before us give us instruction designed to keep us out of the pitfalls of life. They explain what the Torah really meant, and how it applies to our lives. If we disregard their help, and choose to do it "on our own," we're choosing to hamper our own success, and perhaps even to guarantee failure.

The Gemara in *Sotah* (21b–22a) discusses who is a *rasha arum* (a cunning evildoer). The last *peshat*, offered by Ulla, is that this is a person who reads the texts but does not have practical training from a *rav* or *chacham*. He is a *rasha* because his Torah and rulings will be wrong, since he doesn't know how to properly apply what he has learned, and he is deceptive because people will think he is a *talmid chacham* when in reality he is not. In other words, reading a book and thinking you can help yourself is not only foolish, but dangerous and wrong.

Each day, as we face the challenges and opportunities of life, we should turn back to the original guidebook, the Torah, and undertake to learn from others without hesitation, valuing their teachings as a way to ensure our own success.

Hishtadlus without
the Effort

A COUPLE OF WEEKS AGO I had an eye-opening experience. It was a Friday and I was about to enter a supermarket to pick up a few last-minute items. A girl was standing near the entrance selling raffle tickets. I like to encourage these children, so I took the money out of my wallet to buy a ticket, and I also took out a dollar for the man sitting nearby who was collecting money for himself. I figured that I would give her the money and then walk over to him to save him the trouble of getting up.

Well, no sooner had I begun to hand her the money than he came over to me with a big smile, "Good Shabbos!" I gave him the dollar and he walked back to his seat, very pleased with himself.

It struck me. He thinks that it's only because he made the effort to get up and come over to me that he got the dollar. He was making his *hishtadlus* and probably thinks that if he hadn't, he wouldn't have gotten it. How can I assume he thinks that? Because he got up and came over to me.

In this rare instance, though, I had a special insight. I knew that not only was I planning to give him the money, but I was planning to walk over there so he didn't have to get up and exert himself. It was a very surreal perspective, one that the *Ribono shel Olam* has all the time.

He's already determined what we're going to get, and it's ours.

185

It doesn't matter how hard we try or how little we try, we will get it because that has been decreed from above. That being said, we see nothing wrong or futile in spinning our wheels, pushing hard, and exerting ourselves to get what we would have gotten had we remained seated!

"But what do you mean?" you ask. "Everyone knows you have to make *hishtadlus*. Otherwise you won't get anywhere!" Well, you're right and you're wrong.

In *Chovos HaLevavos*, Rabbeinu Bachya ibn Pakuda unequivocally states that our efforts to earn a living mean nothing. We are going to get *what* we're supposed to get, *when* we're supposed to get it. However, there is a point in *hishtadlus*. Two points actually.

You see, *hishtadlus* is a test. You need to work to earn a living. How will you do it? Will you operate according to *halachah*, or will you bend the rules and say, "it's just business"? If you follow *halachah*, you're showing that you choose to be an *oved Hashem*. If you cheat, steal, and all the other wonderful things that people permit for "*parnasah*," then you've shown that you don't trust Hashem to take care of you and you will be repaid accordingly.

I once heard a story about a factory that had been in bankruptcy. The owner told his bookkeeper to backdate orders and vendor invoices so that it appeared they had come in before the bankruptcy in order to avoid paying these vendors. Is this the *derech Hashem*? Or is this factory owner afraid to trust God and figures he has to earn money his own way? He might even be a big *ba'al tzedakah* and buy expensive *aliyos* in shul, but he's still not what Hashem wants him to be.

The second reason to work is that if we didn't have to, we might forget Hashem, as the *pasuk* says, "*Vayishman Yeshurun va'yivat —* Klal Yisrael* got fat and satisfied and kicked at *HaKadosh Baruch Hu*." Thus, the need to work is a preventative measure to keep us from rebelling, or contemplating things we shouldn't and can't fathom, like what was here before the world, and what will be after.

Okay, so we've determined that we really don't need to do *hishtadlus* or be "ambitious" to get what Hashem has prepared for us. Does that mean all our actions are truly fruitless? No.

Our actions are only meaningless as it relates to getting our *parnasah*. However when it comes to *ruchnius*, we can make the effort to gather more and more, even above and beyond what Hashem had prepared for us. The *Navi* says, "Only in this shall the proud be proud, in knowledge and getting to know Me." Our efforts to come closer to Hashem, to improve our negative *middos* and reach for higher levels are the ones which can really bear fruit, and for which a person should feel accomplished. As a bonus, if we do that, then the trouble of striving for *parnasah* goes away too.

That is not to say that you won't have to work for your daily bread, but it doesn't have to feel like work. If your attitude in doing your *hishtadlus* is to show Hashem that you are trying to be righteous and want to do what He commands, then you will feel accomplishment and satisfaction in your efforts and won't feel that you have wasted your time — even if that big deal doesn't pan out.

You will no longer obsess about having to work longer hours or impressing that big client. You will get what's coming to you anyway, so why not focus on impressing the One Who really counts, Who will provide for you in this world and the next? Take the time to learn more of His Torah, to be kind to His children, and become a holy person.

Working doesn't have to be your *hishtadlus*, and *hishtadlus* doesn't have to take a lot of effort. All you need to have is a clear perception of the world and you'll find yourself happier, more satisfied, and a better Jew to boot.

The Observant Jew
Is on Vacation

O KAY, THAT'S WHAT I would have liked to say. Sometimes it
gets very difficult to come up with a topic for my articles. I
figured I could just skip an article and people would understand.
I could tell myself that reports of my loyal readership are greatly
exaggerated — but it would be a cop-out.

I remember when I was in yeshivah in Cleveland and R'
Mordechai Gifter *z"l* was speaking about *bein hazemanim*. More
specifically, he was speaking about a term commonly used to
refer to the long weekends we sometimes had in Telz, and that
are common in other yeshivos too.

The term was "Off-Shabbos." "Off Shabbos?!" the *Rosh Ha-
Yeshivah* exclaimed (which was pretty much the only way he
spoke; always with enthusiasm and fire). "Off?! What are you
'off' from? From the *Ribono shel Olam*?! From *avodas Hashem*?
A Jew never has a day off from Torah and mitzvos! It is a great
joy to learn and do mitzvos, certainly not something you want
to be relieved of!" (Pardon me if I am not exactly quoting the
Rosh HaYeshiva, I am going back many years and this is how I
remember it, based on the impression it made on me.)

This message came back to me when I was working in a camp.
There was a big to-do when some counselors on their "day off"
decided to sleep in and miss *Shacharis*. The question came back

again. "What are you 'off' from? From *davening*? You may be re-lieved of some obligations to watch the campers, but you are still a Jew with an obligation to yourself and Hashem."

So I got to thinking. When I write these articles, what is my responsibility? True, I provide some reading entertainment for some people. Possibly I provide a target of disdain for cynics. But I'm not just a babysitter, entertaining people and keeping them busy. If I were, there'd be nothing wrong with skipping an issue. (Publisher's Note: The writer must have suffered a bout of tempo-rary insanity here. Skip an issue?! Preposterous!)

If that were the case, I could take a week off. But in truth, my articles aim for a higher goal. I try to convey some message, something to think about, some benefit for the world at large. That is a mitzvah. How can I take a week "off" from that? Now, that's not to say that it won't happen at some point when circumstances require it, but it lends a perspective to my actions that makes me think twice about dismissing the job at hand.

I'm sure there are times we all feel like dismissing a respon-sibility. Like getting up on time for *davening*, like returning the shopping cart to the store instead of leaving it in the spot next to us, like having to be sensitive enough not to comment when someone makes a mistake. But these are not optional behaviors; these are mitzvos and obligations.

Even if I'm just giving someone pleasure when they read my articles — is that a small thing? Making someone else happy is a tremendous mitzvah! I have had people tell me they look forward to my articles and enjoy them. Now *that's* a responsibility.

If that's the case, it's not so easy to blow it off. I guess I'll just have to buckle down and figure out something to write about for this week...

The Quicksand Paradox

A T A BOOK SALE one day, I picked up a small volume, about the size of the palm of my hand, entitled, "The Worst-Case Scenario Little Book for Survival." It's filled with tips, tricks, and information for what to do in an emergency such as getting stuck in an elevator or having to jump off a bridge into a river (with the intention of living, of course). The first item in the book talks about how to get out of quicksand. Quicksand is basically a mushy mixture of sand, clay and water, which can be very dangerous. If you step on it, you will start to sink — it only looks solid.

The odd thing about quicksand is that the more pressure you use to pull your feet out, the more it sucks you down. If you want to get out, you need to relax and float. Also, it's important to try to change the angle of your exit. While most of us will never encounter quicksand in our day-to-day lives, I think the Quicksand Paradox is nevertheless very important in everyday existence.

I was speaking to someone who was annoyed. He felt that someone had done something wrong and it bothered him to no end. No matter how much I tried to calm him down, it didn't work. I told him I have a way to get people to do what you want — guaranteed. He was intrigued. "It's simple," I said. "Just change what you want." That's when it hit me — the Quicksand Paradox!

The world is full of things that follow this principle. The more we focus on making ourselves happy, the more unhappy we become. Conversely, the more we focus on making others happy, the happier we find ourselves.

The more "things" a person tries to accumulate, the more "things" there are that he's lacking. The more we have, the more we want. The opposite is true as well, that the less we want, the more we seem to have. The more you try to force someone to your way of thinking, the more they resist. The more you resist change, the more intense the pressure to do so.

Say your spouse does something that drives you batty. Now, I'm not talking about doing something awful, but let's start with something mildly annoying. For example, let's say he or she tells jokes that are simply not funny. It irks you, bothers you, makes you CRAAAAZZZZYYYYY!

You have two choices. Well, one choice actually, if you don't want to do jail time. You can't make them change who they are, but you can change how you feel about it. The more you get annoyed by it, the more it will annoy you. So, if you tell yourself (again and again and again) that it's cute and endearing, you will eventually find it to be so.

A fellow once came to the Steipler with a problem. "My wife is a terrible housekeeper," he lamented. "The house is always dirty, there are things all over the floor, I see dishes in the sink from three days ago. I can't take it anymore; I simply can't live this way. What should I do?"

The Steipler replied, "Take a broom and help!"

The answer is so simple, yet so elusive. He wanted a clean house, but expected his wife to care for the kids, cook meals, and keep his palace sparkling. Well, guess what? She couldn't keep up. Yelling and fighting with her won't make it better, and certainly won't make her want to work harder. But if he wanted a clean house, he could get that by changing his approach. By changing his outlook, and not insisting it was her job, he could go beyond his frustration and be at peace.

Now, I know, someone out there will say, "But it says in *Shulchan Aruch* that the woman's responsibilities include the cooking and cleaning," or "the man has the halachic obligation to support his wife and she doesn't have to work," and that's great if it works out.

But if she can't cope, or his job doesn't pay enough and she needs to work to make ends meet, then it's hurtful to keep pressing the issue. If you want to find happiness, change yourself and make it work.

It's like quicksand. The more you struggle to get your way, the more stuck you will find yourself. On the other hand, if you relax and stop fighting, and perhaps adjust your approach, you may just find yourself rising above the problems.

Don't like the fellow in shul? He acts inappropriately? Guess what — that's not your problem. When you get to *Shamayim* they won't say, "Why didn't you beat him up until he stopped doing X, Y, or Z," they will say, "Why didn't you take control of your anger and pass the test I gave you?"

It's interesting. In the survival book, it says you should always carry a stout stick when in quicksand country. That way, you can put it under your hips, perpendicular to your spine, to help keep you afloat. In other words, if you want to survive, you can't just stick to your own way, you've got to allow for things that don't follow your natural alignment.

Suddenly, I'm thinking that maybe it's not such a paradox. We can't understand why the harder we try to get our way, the stronger the resistance is which tries to keep us from getting it. But maybe that's the whole point. When you lift weights, or use resistance bands, the fact that there's opposition makes you stronger.

Hashem doesn't throw us into quicksand to drown us; He wants us to learn how to cope with disappointment and find other ways to be happy — i.e. *survive*. When we conquer one challenge, another one pops us not because there is no God, but precisely because He's there, watching our progress every step of the way!

So the next time you find yourself sinking into the quagmire of frustration, remind yourself that you can get out easily, simply by changing your attitude. You will find that as you continue to adjust your angle of approach to each situation and accept the curves that life throws at you, your happiness level will rise accordingly. Remember, we may not be here on Earth to conquer the obstacles in front of us; instead, we just might be here to conquer our reactions to them. So relax, and you'll rise to the top every time.

I Know What Regret Looks Like

SOMETHING HAPPENED TO ME last Shabbos that I must write about. The Baal Shem Tov says we never see something unless there's a message for us in it, and I'm hoping to share that message with all my dear readers.

What happened was that Shabbos morning I *davened* in shul with a man who was going to prison in a few days. As I write this, the news headlines talk about this man who was once powerful, but whose name is now a source of anguish for the many who had dealings with him.

I don't condone what he was accused of doing, nor am I interested. Some may say his white-collar crimes were awful, while some may say they are par for the course where he comes from. None of that matters. Why? Because when a person does *teshuvah*, we don't remind him of his past. Also, unless a person has done harm directly to me, it is not my business, nor am I allowed to believe *lashon hara* about him. Even if he did harm to me, I'm not allowed to discuss it and pontificate about it. In the meantime, however, let's get to the point of my article.

As I watched this man *daven* with intensity, listening to the *rav*'s *derashah*, and seeming to bask in the *kedushah* of shul, I was struck by the expressions on his face. At times, his expression became pained, contorted with emotion. I could imagine him willing to forgo all the millions he made and years of power he wielded for a few minutes more of *Yiddishkeit* and closeness to Hashem.

At what was more than likely his last Shabbos with a *minyan* for the next seventy months, he didn't talk and joke. He was somber, and keenly aware of his surroundings. Someone in the community told me that for the past several weeks leading up to his incarceration, he has seemed to be trying to grasp every drop of *kedushah* possible, almost drinking it in through his skin.

It got me to thinking. Do you think he regrets what he did to get where he is today? Do you think he regrets spending his time as he did? Do you think he now has much better priorities and an understanding of what's really important? I think so. And because I witnessed him, I think I do too.

This man is going to prison for earthly crimes. He knew which day he would be escorted to prison, and had at least some time to prepare himself. He had time to reflect on what he had given up with his poor choices and how his decisions affected his family and those around him. He has regret, but when he is released, he will *iy"H* have an opportunity to live life the way he should have all along.

We never know when we will be escorted from this world, nor what is waiting for us there. Once we go, we have no more opportunity to live the life we should have. Imagine how much regret there will be for lost opportunities and wasted minutes, days, months, and years. The Vilna Gaon writes that the ultimate suffering takes place at the moment of death when the veil is lifted and a person sees all they could have achieved but didn't.

The lesson I learned is that regret is possible in this lifetime. We should feel it ourselves, and look to make ourselves right with our decisions. We should take the opportunities we have to live and learn and love. We should tell the people we care about that we're happy they're in our lives, and call friends we haven't spoken with in a while who would be happy to hear from us.

We should take advantage of *davening* and not waste it by chatting with our friends and neighbors (especially NOT about politics!) as if we had all the time in the world. Learning should not mean we focus on the coffee and cake, but on communing with Hashem and drinking in His words.

I hope that the inspiration borne of this article will stand in good stead as a *zechus* for this fellow, through whom I was inspired. The lesson he taught us all is simple: If we live our lives aware of the ultimate regret, then, at the end, when we are escorted to the Final Judgment, we will have no regrets at all.

The Importance of Mitzvah Notes

*U*NTIL A FEW YEARS AGO, I had never heard of a mitzvah note. Growing up in New Orleans we didn't have such things as a mitzvah note. Nor did we have *Pirchei*, Paskesz, or Uncle Moishy. The closest thing I can remember was when Shlomo Carlebach came to town. I can still recall the struggling expression on his face trying to explain what a *chassid* was to a group of kids who thought of Purim as the "Jewish version of Mardi Gras."

When I did hear about mitzvah notes, I didn't understand the concept. You are supposed to do mitzvos, why do you need a bribe to get you to do them? Kids should be good because that's what they're supposed to do. Isn't it the wrong message teaching them that you have to be rewarded for every little thing?

That's what I used to think. But then I got a little older... a little wiser... a little daughter.

Okay, at first, I still thought that way. When my daughter asked me for mitzvah notes I grudgingly gave them. Of course, sometimes I wanted to give her notes because she did exceptional things. But for run-of-the-mill stuff, like brushing her teeth and sharing, I didn't jump to do it. What was the big deal? I mean, all that happened was that the teacher would look at it, maybe give her a smiley face sticker, and that's that, right?

At the end of the year, when I went to her class graduation, the teacher had arranged a special display of each child's mitzvah notes. It was clear for everyone to see who had notes. Some had bunches; one unfortunate child had only one. *Baruch Hashem*, our daughter was somewhere in the middle, but that stark sight of the lone mitzvah-note struck me.

What message would the child take from it? That his or her parents didn't have time for him or her? (I'm not giving any hints; if it's your child, you know who you are.) Maybe *chas v'shalom* that there was only one time in the year when Mommy and Daddy were proud enough to write? It was heartbreaking.

This year, my second daughter entered Nursery and the teacher sent home special mitzvah-note paper. I dutifully scribbled notes for my girls for the first few days of school. Then I saw her class schedule and was startled.

During snack, the kids eat and listen to mitzvah notes from the other children! Oh my goodness! What if I didn't send any notes? What if all year my child listened to everyone else's notes and never her own? How terrible would she feel?

Forgetting about the negative feelings, this means that the notes are really important in another way. Not only will my daughter hear her note read by her teacher, whom she looks up to (she has to, I mean, she's only two feet tall), but her friends will hear it too. They will know that her parents think she is worthy of complimenting and her esteem will likely go up in their eyes. This is such an awesome responsibility to have. I have to ensure that she is getting enough positive reinforcement and open expression of the deep love I have for her.

Back to my original premise. I said that a note was merely a bribe to get a child to do something and there was no reason to have to write a note and compliment for things they are supposed to do anyway. Let's look at the flip side. If my child did something wrong, would I say, "*Nu*, she's a kid, she's supposed to write on the walls," or would I chastise her and let her know she did something wrong? "How else will she learn?" I think we all know the answer.

So let's get this straight: Every time our children do wrong, we tell them. When they do right, we expect it and remain silent. That doesn't seem fair to me. If anything, when they do wrong (childish mistakes like spilling things, accidents, etc.), we should expect it and remain silent, or perhaps even encourage them, reassure them, and tell them that things will get easier as they grow up.

When they do what they're "supposed to do" we should compliment them, tell them how proud we are, and yes, write mitzvah notes.

Now, let's ask ourselves — does this need for approval ever go away? Do we ever get to the point where we don't at least like to hear that others love us, appreciate us, and admire us? The answer is obviously no. We all need the reassurances of others that we've done a good job or make them feel good or that they are happy we exist in their lives.

It would make sense, then, that while we don't write mitzvah notes for grown-ups, we should be in the habit of telling our spouses, friends, co-workers, and neighbors when they do things right. Come to think of it, we can write mitzvah notes. If someone gives you a gift, write a thank-you note instead of just calling. (Of course you were going to say thank you, weren't you?) If a co-worker sends you a document that's well written, why not respond with a compliment and cc the others to whom it was sent? Writing a note or e-mail to a spouse about something nice they did for you will mean a tremendous amount to them, and will probably result in them doing even nicer things.

Continuing with this theory, it would also make sense to overlook the shortcomings of others and chalk it up to being human. NEWSFLASH: Human beings have flaws.

So, if someone does something insensitive to you, assume they weren't maliciously trying to hurt you. They're people. More than likely they weren't even thinking about you. Maybe one day they'll grow up and change, but until then, don't sweat it. If someone does something stupid, I bet they already know it and don't need you to point it out. If you hold your tongue, odds are next time they need help or advice you're the one they will turn to because you aren't judgmental to them.

Yes, mitzvah notes are very important. Whenever you get the chance, focus on what's "write" in the world, and pretty soon you will notice a whole lot more smiley faces around you.

Life Hangs in the Balance

T HERE IS A CERTAIN shul I attend on occasion where the *rav* never
fails to make some reference to my articles. Almost as soon as
I enter the foyer of the shul, he says, "You don't have to include this
in an article," or "I hope you don't write an article about that."

What's funny is that each time this happens, something I deem
worthy of being written occurs. This time, it was something I said
that I didn't intend to be profound, yet the way it came out made
me decide it should be written down.

On that morning, I was given *Hagbah* (the honor of lifting the
sefer Torah in the air, showing it to the attendees, then sitting with
it upright, ready to be tied and covered). As we had *leined* the last
parshah in the Torah, *V'zos HaBerachah*, the *sefer Torah* was rolled
almost entirely to one side. As I approached, murmured comments
offered opinions on how difficult it would be, musing whether I
was a righty or a lefty, including the *de rigueur* comments about
having eaten my Wheaties.

I managed a smooth lift, opened the Torah about four columns
wide, and turned completely around. The Rabbi whispered, "I
knew you could do it." That's when the following pearl of wisdom
fell from my lips: "It's not about strength; it's about balance."

In truth, this is really the secret to a good *Hagbah*. It's not
a question of how strong you are, though if it's a heavy scroll, a
weakling might not be able to lift it. The lift itself isn't so bad. The
hard part is getting it into the open position and keeping it from

flopping over. That is achieved by making sure the parchment is taut, so that you're lifting one large item with both hands, not trying to control two individual scrolls, one in each hand.

If you've never done *Hagbah,* you probably have no idea what I'm talking about, so I've just eliminated at least half my readership if not more. But suffice it to say that when people think big muscles guarantee success, they're dead wrong.

Often, we try to get our way or make our points by screaming louder than the other person, or by getting angry and showing powerful emotion. We think this will impress them and help us. The odds are it actually works against us.

You see, as much as we want to be right, so does our opponent; be they our friend, enemy, business partner, neighbor or spouse. Strength may make a person give in, but it won't make them agree with you. For that, you need diplomacy and balance.

You need to find a way for them to feel that they got their way, or at least that they weren't totally stripped of any options or opinions. If something is forced, it won't last.

I'm reminded of an old parable from a Sunday School book my mother used to teach from. The sun and the wind made a wager about who could get a man to take off his coat. The wind tried first, blowing with all his might. Fierce wind swirled around the poor man, but he just pulled his coat around himself more tightly. The wind blew until he was blue in the face...or blew in the face... or whatever... but he could not get the man to take off his coat.

Then it was the sun's turn. Instead of force, he just beamed at the fellow until he felt all warm and cozy. Then he kept on smiling and the man got hot, ultimately removing his jacket.

I guess it's pretty simple. Force isn't all it's cracked up to be. Imagine your child tells you he can't sleep. Do you think a calm lullaby will work? Or would it perhaps be better if you berated him for ten minutes at the top of your lungs about how he will be too tired to go to school or have fun or do anything else, and if he doesn't go to sleep this instant he will never be allowed to see his friends and he will end up a sanitation engineer in a small town in Appalachia? I think we know which one has a better chance of working.

How about yelling at someone who is hysterical: "CALM DOWN THIS SECOND OR YOU'LL BE SORRY!!!"? Think it will work? I don't.

The problem is, it takes more strength to remain balanced than to exhibit strength and force. Ironically, showing our power is one of the easiest things for us to do, while being calm and soft is so much harder.

"It's not about strength, it's about balance."

If we can remember that, then we have a better chance of succeeding in our goals and of uplifting others (and the *sefer Torah*). It doesn't matter whether or not you've eaten your Wheaties; you can be a champion every time.

My Own Private Everest

*I*N 1924, WHEN BRITISH mountain climber George Mallory was asked why he wanted to climb Mt. Everest, he famously replied, "Because it's there." In August of that year, attempting to summit Everest, Mallory and his climbing partner Andrew Irvine disappeared. It wasn't until nearly thirty years later that Sir Edmund Hillary actually climbed Mount Everest and lived to talk about it. Clearly, just because you see something is there, doesn't mean that you're the one to conquer it.

Which brings me to a conversation I overheard in shul last week. "The Torah doesn't say anything about what made Moshe Rabbeinu special and worthy to lead the Jewish People. Sure, the *midrash* says different things, but the *pesukim* don't tell us why he was chosen."

We are all familiar with the famous *midrash* relating how Moshe was tending his flocks and one little lamb ran away. Moshe ran after it a great distance until it came to a spring of water. He said, "*Oy*, you poor *shep'se'leh*. If I had known you were thirsty I would have given you a drink. You ran so far…" He then put the little lamb on his shoulders and carried it back to the flock. It was then that Hashem said, "Moshe has shown such compassion for his flock, he will now lead Mine."

That's a wonderful story but it's not in the actual written Torah. The closest thing we find to any reason for his being chosen was when Hashem showed Moshe the burning bush and "Hashem saw that he turned to look." True, *Chazal* speak about his constant interest in the Jews and the fact that he was concerned for their welfare, and considered the Jews his brothers even though he was raised in the palace, but the most we find is that Moshe may have been curious about the sight he saw.

I told the fellow who asked this question that he was going to be in my article this week because he gave me a fabulous insight. Moshe said to Hashem, "*Shelach na b'yad tishlach* — Send someone more appropriate." Hashem's response was that He had chosen Moshe. He gives people their abilities and the appropriate choice was made. In his humility, Moshe may have felt unprepared or unworthy, but Hashem told him that he was ready.

So now, let's go back to the question. If all these events happened, as related by the *midrash* and *Chazal*, why were they not in the Torah? The Torah doesn't give us any reason for Moshe being chosen other than, "Because I said so." Perhaps, that's exactly the point. Moshe Rabbeinu had developed himself into a man worthy of leadership through a string of smaller exercises and tests, pushing himself to the high levels he attained. However, these subtle changes went unnoticed by him, and he felt as humble as ever.

When Hashem chose him and he demurred, Hashem said, "I know you are the right man for the job even if you don't." The reasons he was up to the task are not recorded in the Torah because none of us clearly sees the marks of greatness and recognizes the challenges we've overcome to get where we are. It's never clear-cut and obvious.

Instead, we have to take Hashem's word for it that if He brought us to a place or situation, it's because He knows we're ready, even if we don't. George Mallory may have wanted to summit Everest, but he didn't because that wasn't what Hashem wanted from him. God brought Edmund Hillary to Everest in 1953 because *he* was the one who was supposed to be the first to climb it.

I guess you could say Mallory was close, but had it wrong: You don't climb Everest because IT'S there… You summit mountains because YOU are there.

The Dangers of
Going "On Line"

*I*F WHEN YOU READ the title of this article you thought I was going to talk about the Internet, then you already know about the pitfalls of unlimited access, and I can talk about what I really wanted to talk about, which is something we do all the time.

It may be at the bank or the supermarket, in our cars or on foot, both men and women, and even children. At some point, we will have to stand in line. Historically, some places had a line painted on the floor to show people where to stand, hence the term waiting "on line." Of course, if you're British, you know all this, as you undoubtedly have a high "I queue."

Recently I had the unpleasant experience of attempting to pick up some food from a restaurant on an unusually busy day. It seems that a number of other people had also ordered food, and the kitchen staff couldn't keep up. As I walked in, I was the fifteenth or sixteenth person on line. People were grumbling. Then it got louder. People got angry. I stayed calm.

It's not that my time isn't valuable; it's not that I enjoy waiting. It's that I realized the simple facts of the circumstances in which I found myself. I was there to pick up take-out food. That means that I could afford food, and that I could afford *restaurant* food. The woman outside collecting *tzedakah* to pay for her daughter's operation wasn't grumbling about the line because it didn't affect her.

Often we go to a bank and get annoyed because we're waiting on line. But the fact that we're there means we have money, and shouldn't we be thankful for that?

Upset by the lines at the airport? You are blessed enough to be able to travel and you're whining because it takes a few extra minutes?

First of all, as we've said in the past about traffic, how long it's going to take you is determined not by you or the driver ahead of you or the cashier or the teller at the counter. It's determined by *HaKadosh Baruch Hu*. Don't believe me? Try finding the shortest line at the grocery store. If you think you're able to control the world so the woman with only one item in front of you won't need a price check then attempt to pay with a personal check from a bank in an obscure third-world country, think again. These things happen and there's not a thing you can do about it.

What you *can* do is adjust your attitude. In NASA lingo, attitude control is the term which basically refers to the direction a spacecraft is pointed. Even a tiny error in attitude and it can go millions of miles off course. For us, attitude control is just as important, and refers to how we feel about the situations we're in. If we have the wrong attitude, we can wind up hopelessly off course.

You can control your attitude; I just did it. Once again, I'm writing this article while waiting for my car. This time, I'm getting the tires rotated. They told me it would take an hour. That was an hour ago. I just asked the guy at the counter and he said they'll take it in in two minutes and be done in ten. That's really frustrating because I have to get to work. But then something hit me.

What am I writing? That it's not in my control. All I can control is how I react. So, *Baruch Hashem*, they're bringing my car in, and it was not Divinely ordained to be in a minute earlier. I can yell and scream and get upset, but that won't turn back the clock. I actually have to thank all of you because if not for the fact that I knew you'd be reading this article and it would make me a hypocrite not to listen to my own advice, I probably would have made the mistake of not being grateful that I have a car, or a job I need to get to, or forgetting that the person behind the counter isn't necessarily responsible for the delay.

When you're in line or have to wait for your wife or children to finish getting ready to go somewhere, think about what it means. Whether it means you have money, food, or a family, you're tremendously blessed. Take a moment to thank Hashem for what you have. There's a story about someone who complained to the Satmar Rav about all the *meshulachim* and beggars who came to his door asking for *tzedakah*. The Rav responded, "I give you my blessing that you should always remain on that side of the door." How's that for a reality check?

Plus, if you can keep yourself calm, you'll be rewarded for controlling your temper, and you won't say things you'll regret later. And, perhaps, if you've learned all your lessons about waiting in line, Hashem won't have to keep sending them to you.

So, the next time the guy in the turning lane ahead of you sits there at the red light, then sheepishly turns on his blinker to get into the non-turning lane, take a deep breath, sit back, and thank God that one more test is behind you.

The Bitachon Machine

*H*AVE YOU EVER WISHED you could invent a tool for fulfilling mitzvos? Maybe a *zitzfleish* device that would let you manage to sit still long enough to hear a *shiur* or learn a *blatt gemara*? That would be pretty cool. How about a gadget that would give you a small electric shock every time you spoke *lashon hara*? Okay, you'd probably need to change the batteries too often... but the idea has merit.

Maybe these inventions haven't been created yet, but every piece of technology has a purpose and there's one that we've fallen in love with almost universally. I'm talking about, of course, the GPS. Officially it stands for "Global Positioning System," the network of satellites used to determine the location of the unit and cross-reference those coordinates on a map to get us from point A to point B, but it could just as well stand for "God Protect us from Stupidity."

We've all heard the story of the German couple who drove past a sign stating the road was closed only to plunge into a river because the GPS told them to because it didn't know the bridge had been washed away in a storm, and we've nearly all got our own horror stories. Like the fellow who asked his GPS to find him the fastest route from Monsey to Baltimore making the best use of freeways. (He chose to ignore the clear directions given to him by someone who had done the trip numerous times.) He found himself in Allentown, Pennsylvania two hours later because GPS translated "freeways" to exclude toll roads like the Garden State Parkway and New Jersey Turnpike. (Incidentally, this was the same fellow who asked me if I was sure I knew my own address because according to his GPS my house number didn't exist.)

Or think of the fellow who followed the somewhat dubious set of twists and turns dictated by his GPS only to pull up to an abandoned warehouse and have his mechanical map joyfully announce, "You have arrived at your destination!" So, maybe people need to use their own judgment a little when utilizing this device, but it got me to thinking (and what doesn't?).

The Chafetz Chaim is quoted as saying that from each technological advance we can learn something. From a telephone, that what you say here is heard over there. From a film, that what you do can be recorded and replayed somewhere else at a later time. From a train, that in one moment you can miss it all. As technology advances, and huge amounts of data are beamed instantly through space and transmitted invisibly over thousands of miles, these messages are all the more intensified.

So I asked myself, what about the GPS? What lesson is there in that?

I think I know what it is — blind faith. To be more precise, *bitachon*.

You see, if I don't know where I'm going, but I know where I want to end up, I will ask for directions. I'll check a map, ask someone who knows, and get ready for the trip. But what if I don't have anyone to ask or I am suddenly faced with a fork in the road? What do I do then?

That's when I trust my GPS. I believe that it has more knowledge of the roads than I do. Though I don't know exactly how it will get me to my destination, I trust it to do just that.

Now let's parallel that to *bitachon*. I have goals; I have desires. I look to the Torah and my rabbis and teachers for guidance. But there are times when I am faced with a situation that I don't have previous experience with. Or better yet, I disagree with the data I've gotten because I imagine the map (read: Torah) I checked is outdated or the roads have changed since the last time the person giving me directions (read: rabbi) traveled them. For example, to some (ok, most people) it doesn't make logical sense to be able to make a *parnasah* without cheating or cutting corners. You do what you have to do.

Well, what would the GPS tell us if we wanted to get someplace we weren't sure how to reach? Even if it wasn't logical, we would remind ourselves that there is a lot more knowledge rolled up in that little guy than we have and if it thinks it can get us where we need to go, we ought to follow its advice.

That's building our *bitachon* muscles. By being able to let go and realize we are not all-knowing, we are better able to understand that Hashem doesn't work by human logic. He gets us where we need to be because it is God Who orchestrates every action in the world and puts everything on earth in its place.

Following the Torah as if it were a GPS is like having our own personal *bitachon* trainer rolled up in a little plastic box. Now, if someone invented a machine like that, and I had to name this device, which helps us remember that God knows His way around the world better than we do and we ought to follow His directions, I think I'd call it… I'd call it… well, I guess I'd call it a Global Positioning System.

A Light unto
the Nations

THE *NAVI* YESHAYAHU (42:6) tells us that Hashem has established us, the Jewish People, as a light unto the nations, who represent God to the world by our exemplary lifestyle, and imbue the world with knowledge of His existence.

We live amongst the nations of the world, often despised, frequently ridiculed, but always watched and studied. When we make a *kiddush Hashem*, ascribing glory to His name, we have done our duty, but often with little fanfare.

When we stumble, our mistakes are often rebroadcast in the media and in the hearts and minds of the nations we are trying to impress and inspire by living as we are commanded to live. We must be ever-vigilant, therefore, that we act as we should, and live up to the greatness that is inside each and every one of us.

Chasidah

*I*T'S AMAZING HOW HELPFUL people want to be. I had someone call me up to give me an idea for an article because he saw that I wrote how hard it can be to come up with ideas. Well, he was rather hot under the collar and steamed about an incident that took place. He wanted me to badmouth people who are selfish and don't care about other people. I can't do that in good conscience. *Klal Yisrael* is a nation of good people. There are enough people badmouthing us that I don't need to do it too.

For example, take his situation. He was driving down a small residential street. The driver of the car ahead of him stopped and called a greeting to a neighbor raking leaves in his driveway. The neighbor stopped raking and approached the car to chat. Our friend lightly leaned on his horn to alert them that he was there. The talkers, sensing his objection, instantly reacted and gave him a look of, "Can't you see I'm talking?! What chutzpah you have to honk!"

He saw that as bad *middos*. I say it shows what *ahavas Yisrael* they have. I mean, to totally be oblivious to everything else in the world because you are talking to a beloved fellow Jew... that's amazing. It shows how important your friend is to you. What could be wrong with that?

Take another example. The school bus pulls up and stops traffic in both directions. The mothers of these children, out of protective love for their young offspring, want to ensure the bus comes to a complete stop before getting their child's coat on and sending them back to the hall closet to get their backpacks.

Our friend would want them to realize that other people are waiting to pass and it's unfair to make them sit there immobile for the three to four minutes this whole procedure takes, and have the child ready and waiting to board the bus. Obviously, that's because he is not keenly concerned about children's safety. However, our vigilant parent makes sure the child is not subjected to the strain of waiting for the bus on top of the stress of school. Such parental love; and yet, some people don't see the beauty of it.

In fact, you are likely to find these mothers in the supermarket. You can spot them because they wait until everything is packed and the cashier is waiting with the total to begin unzipping their pocketbooks and searching for their checkbooks. Why? Well, they wouldn't want that poor cashier to feel pressured that the customer was waiting for her, would they? And forget about finding a pen for their checkbook or filling out the store's name on the check — the cashier might get flustered and scan something wrong, causing her to void it and rescan! How awful. No, this woman calmly waits for the order to be complete.

In fact, to make the transaction completely stress-free for the cashier, this woman may have a loud conversation with a woman in the next checkout aisle to show that she is oblivious to what's going on at her own checkout register.

There is precedent for this behavior in the Torah. The Torah lists various types of birds, one of which is called the *chasidah*, meaning the kind or pious one. *Chazal* tell us that this bird cares deeply about its family and close friends and ensures that they have what they need. The problem is that this bird is *chazer-treif* (forbidden to eat)!

Because it only thinks about those it is close to, without thinking about the wider world around them, its kindness is severely deformed and misplaced. That can probably be the explanation for the behavior of people like our "rake-on" from earlier. He does love his fellow Jews, but only when they're HIS fellow Jews. As far as he's concerned, the rest of us can fly south for the winter. Far south.

It is an emulation of this bird that we find when people "reserve" parking spaces for their friends by leaving the shopping carts in the spots closest to the store when they leave. Similar to leaning a chair up at a dinner, this method of reservation ensures that nobody else can take that spot.

Wait, you tell me you're *not* reserving the parking space for anyone?! Even when you leave your shopping cart in a spot instead of taking the extra fifteen to twenty seconds to return it to the front of the store?! Then you're even worse than the *chasidah*! At least she thinks of some of her fine-feathered fellows; you're only thinking about yourself!

Well, I think that's probably what our friend who suggested that topic for this column would say. But I'm not going to. No way. I care too much about people's feelings to say anything. I'm just going to keep my mouth shut and let people figure it out for themselves.

Not Seeing the Forest for the "ME"s

*W*HEN I WAS IN yeshivah in Cleveland, a new store opened up nearby which revolutionized Thursday nights. This 24-hour supercenter predated and surpassed Super Wal-Marts. Not only did they have a full department store, grocery store, and low prices, but they actually had people on the registers to ring you up when you wanted to pay!

For us in yeshivah, it was a boon. You could learn late Thursday night, then head over to TwinValu for your Shabbos shopping at 2 A.M. It was amazing.

One night, as I casually perused the merchandise on various aisles, I saw one of the stock boys pass me. He was obviously somewhat mentally challenged, and was having a rather animated conversation as he walked passed me. Now, today, this is a common sight, but my experience at the store was before the days of cell-phone headsets that fit in your ear so I knew he wasn't on the phone.

To no one in particular, I said, "Wow, look at that poor guy. Wandering aimlessly through the store, talking to himself..."

...a moment later I said, "But then again, so am I."

When it came to "ME," I understood that I wasn't crazy, but looking at someone else, I didn't see things quite the same way. Sometimes, I think we find ourselves talking to other people, trying to make them understand, but we're really just talking to ourselves. (No, ladies, I don't mean when you're trying to have a conversation with your husband.)

I mean when we're in the car for example, and someone cuts us off. Often we can be heard to say such niceties as, "Pardon me, sir, I didn't realize I was driving so slowly." Or else we might say, "Oh, I see you must have more important things to do than I, and I'm glad you took the opportunity to get ahead of me." Isn't that what you say?

Now, admittedly, I have heard people somewhat more agitated than that. I recall one driver lovingly beseeching the other drivers to speed up a tad with, "COME ON PEOPLE, I DON'T *LIVE* FOR YOU!"

We know they can't hear us, but if they do something wrong, we just have to cry out. That happened to me recently as I entered a parking lot one rainy day.

As I headed to my store of choice, I stopped to let an older couple cross in front of me. It was raining, and the fellow was holding a large, black, golf umbrella. That was not out of the ordinary, but what happened next infuriated me. He and his wife left the car from their respective sides. At the front of the car, they moved closer together, and then he proceeded to cross to the storefronts, leaving his wife behind! As an older woman, she seemed to move a bit more slowly, and while he carried this large umbrella, she walked slowly in the rain. "WHAT'S WRONG WITH YOU?! HOLD THE UMBRELLA OVER HER! HELLO? SHE'S YOUR WIFE AND SHE'S GETTING WET! WHERE ARE YOU GOING?!" I don't think he heard me, but I couldn't control it.

What is the point of having an umbrella if your wife is going to get wet? If it were me, I would have walked around to her side before she got out to make sure she stayed dry and that's not just because she frequently reminds me that her hair costs a lot more than mine does. And if the umbrella wasn't large enough for both of us, I would still carry it over her. How can I possibly stay dry at someone else's expense? How could this fellow have been so blind?

I think it's a case of not seeing the forest for the "ME"s. We get so caught up worrying about ourselves that we forget about other people. We leave the shopping carts in the handicapped space or just shove them towards the store because we're in a hurry, without thinking that someone else will have to move them. Sometimes, the *Ribono shel Olam* has some fun with these people and they back out of the space only to bump into their own hapless cart and knock out a taillight. They get angry but they've nobody to blame but themselves. They got harmed because they didn't care enough about someone else.

I could go on and on, but I won't. We all know countless examples we can find where we get a little bit selfish. Like when we stand and eat in front of the buffet table at a *Kiddush*, so we can get our second plate (ok, third, but who's counting). Maybe someone else wants to get in there and get some food? "But if he does, he might take the rest of that amazing cake and I won't have any more!" That's selfish. That's people. That's "ME."

I had a friend who calls this "BNH syndrome." These are people who take "*Bi'shvili nivra ha-olam* — The world was created for me" to the extreme. They forget that everyone else is supposed to say that too. But what does it mean?

I once heard a beautiful explanation of *anavah* (humility) from R' Yisrael Reisman in one of his *Navi shiurim*. I don't recall whom he quoted but the concept stayed with me. He said that the word "*anav*," typically translated as a "humble person" comes from the root of "*ana*," meaning, "to answer." An *anav*, therefore, is someone who is selfless, and is always answering the needs of others.

He doesn't see buying a larger umbrella as a tool for keeping himself dry; he chooses it as a means to help someone else. The *anav* doesn't stand on the mat drying his feet when there is someone behind him in the cold. If he hasn't let the other person in first, at least he moves out of the way. He's the one who makes sure his shopping cart isn't blocking the aisle while he decides which cookies to buy. He's the one who has a harder time seeing himself than seeing others.

He is what I can be, when I stop looking out for "ME."

Give 'Til It Feels Good

Manufacturer's Warning: Do NOT read this article in the bathtub or any other place you are not allowed to learn Torah. You've been warned!

*H*OW MANY TIMES HAVE you heard someone making an appeal use the phrase "give 'til it hurts"? Is that supposed to motivate me somehow? Does he think I have one of those gag wallets that gives you an electric shock when you open it? What on earth does that mean?

Now, in truth, I know exactly what he means. He wants us to extend ourselves, and stretch beyond the point where we feel comfortable, to where we are uncomfortable about giving so much. That's how he plans to get the big bucks. As my *Rosh HaYeshivah* R' Gifter *z"l* would say — BUNK! (It means, "nonsense!" or at least that's what I think he meant when he said it...)

I do agree that we often give as much as we feel comfortable giving, and that perhaps we could do more. But is comparing *tzedakah* to root canal going to inspire me to give generously? I think not. When I write a check should I plan to experience a searing pain in my cerebral cortex? I don't think so.

Instead, I would say that what we need to do is give 'til it feels good. If you can easily afford an $18 donation for example, pushing yourself to $36 is a bit harder, but very rewarding. If you then go to $50 (for a worthy cause, of course), which makes you stop and think because you don't throw that kind of money around, then you can start to feel good about what you've given. It makes an impact on you that you managed to realize what money is for and do with it what Hashem intended. Of course, if $50 is what you normally tip the guy who washes your car, the stakes are higher.

An acquaintance of mine married the daughter of a very wealthy man. Throughout the planning for the wedding, he kept telling his future father-in-law that he wanted to keep it simple. Finally, his *shver*-to-be told him, "I want you to know, whatever I spend on your wedding, I'm giving an equal amount to marry off orphans in Eretz Yisrael." Wow! Who would think like that? Only someone who knows why he was given wealth. Now, some naysayers may be thinking, sure, when you're rich you can do that sort of thing.

Ahh.… Obviously you haven't reviewed the Gemara in *Bava Basra* (9b, as I'm sure you'll want to look it up) which says that one who runs after *tzedakah* will find himself given more money, in order to give more *tzedakah*. In essence, one who is a good fund manager for Hashem and invests wisely will be given more money to handle.

So the question is: How much is the right amount to give? Don't we need to be worried about overextending ourselves? Or better yet, you're ready to overextend yourself, but you say, "How do I know that the person really needs the money? Maybe he's a faker and I won't get credit for this donation?"

That's a good question, and that's why the Gemara continues by saying that one who pursues *tzedakah* opportunities will be presented with worthy recipients. If you're trying to give, Hashem makes it easy. You have to want to give though, which is where the feeling good part comes in.

A while back, someone asked me for a sizable amount of money. I was taken aback, and asked if it was a loan. He explained that in his position, he had no way to pay it back, so no, it wasn't a loan. I said I'd think about it.

I did think about it. It was a large amount for me, but I had some money put away just then and I figured, "What am I saving it for? Maybe just for this." I gave him the money. Two weeks later, I lost my job.

I went back to him and said, "I want to thank you. Had you asked me for the money two weeks later, I wouldn't have given it to you because of my uncertain future. *Baruch Hashem* I was *zocheh* to give it to you." I can't describe how it felt to have given the money. It was like getting in on a great opportunity at just the last second. It felt good. Really good.

Other times I have hyper-extended myself, rationalizing, "If I don't feel that I gave anything, did I really?" I can't think of a single time the *Ribono shel Olam* didn't shower back *berachah* on me. And why not? I was an excellent fund manager, investing where He would want me to!

You, too, can be a high-rolling fund manager for *HaKadosh Baruch Hu*, by being a little more aggressive in your finances and taking some risks. If you think that by giving more you might feel a pinch down the road, think about what you might do if you had a business opportunity that required you to scrimp for a while, but enjoy the benefits later.

Most people would do it even if there was just a 60% to 70% chance of success. Here, it's 100% guaranteed, backed by the full faith of the *Ribono shel Olam*.

What Did You Call Me?!

WHEN I WAS IN yeshivah, I used to get annoyed when I went to *simchah*s with place cards. While my friends who were younger than I, but married, had place cards that read Rabbi K..., and Rabbi H..., mine invariably read Yonason Gwertz (which should really be YeHOnason, and don't get me started on Gewirtz...) or simply Jonny. It especially bothered me after I was halfway to getting my *semichah*. "I am closer to being a rabbi than these guys," I would think to myself. "Just because they're married they get treated differently?"

The truth is, there was good precedent for such treatment. I heard that the Alter of Slabodka would ask a new person in the *beis midrash*, "*Bist du a bachur, oder zeit ir a yungerman?*" He used the more respectful Yiddish word for you — *ir* — if they were married.

As I got older, I realized that the name didn't mean that much. It got to a point where I told the *gabbai* in shul only to call me HaRav if my mother or mother-in-law were present. I realized that to really deserve the name, I had to learn and do so much more. (Though sometimes when I make a *MiShebeirach* for my daughters I will say, *bas HaRav...* — as it's never too early to start thinking about *shidduchim*.)

Some time ago, *Klal Yisrael* and the world were shaken by the tremendous *chillul Hashem* perpetrated with the announcement that numerous people were arrested for various illegal activities, "among them rabbis and politicians."

Unfortunately, many people weren't as upset that the name of *HaKadosh Baruch Hu* was tarnished as they were that the media "automatically calls anyone with a yarmulke a 'rabbi.'" People railed against the anti-Semitism, the yellow journalism, and the chutzpah. I didn't get it. It seemed to me that there were rabbis among the people who were arrested, so why was everyone upset about that?

I think the problem is a larger issue. These people are upset about laypeople being called rabbis because if every Jew was a rabbi, then EVERYONE would have to live up to a higher standard, including them! These people who spend their time gossiping, accusing, wasting precious moments and doing very un-Jewish things might themselves one day be called rabbis and that would be terrible.

I mentioned to a friend that in a nursing home one day, an elderly woman greeted me with a, "Good afternoon, Rabbi." He was incensed.

"You should tell her, 'I'm sorry, I'm not a rabbi.'"

"Why?" I asked.

"Because a rabbi is a higher level," he fumed, "they have higher standards."

I beg to differ. As I understood it, in the non-Jewish world, a priest is holy, the average people are not. When you want to get a little holiness you go to the priest (*Rachmana litzlan*) and then you go back to being yourself. But as *Yidden*, we are *all* holy. A rabbi is just someone who is more knowledgeable and is capable of teaching you how to be holy, like he is. The word "rabbi" means master or teacher, not priest.

Correct me if I'm wrong, but R' Moshe Feinstein *z"l* didn't have a bigger *chiyuv* than me to put on *tefillin*, and the Chafetz Chaim *z"l* wasn't commanded to watch his tongue any more than me. Of course, the larger the stature the greater the responsibility to prevent even the remotest possibility of a person believing some impropriety took place, as it can cause a greater *chillul Hashem*, but basic *halachah* is the same for all of us.

The story is famously told of R' Shimon Schwab *z"l* who was told that a *frum Yid* stole some money and was going to jail. R' Schwab said it wasn't true. When the fellow assured it that it was an actual occurrence, the sage responded, "It can't be true. If he stole money, he's not a FRUM Jew!"

Now, getting back to the way "*frum*" Jews are portrayed in the media when they get caught doing something wrong, or even if they are innocent, but it's perceived that they did something wrong, let's look at what they're really saying. When they say, "Bernie Green, a Jew from New York, was arrested for embezzling seventy million dollars," we complain that they wouldn't say, "Albert O'Toole, an Irish Catholic, was arrested for blowing up a church." But why do they focus on our being Jewish? For the same reason they may call someone a rabbi even when he doesn't have *semichah*, like my friends at the weddings.

When my friends were called rabbi, it was a sign of respect. These were people who were learning in *kollel*, who dedicated their lives to serving Hashem. Even if technically they weren't rabbis, they represented what it means to be a rabbi. Whoever wrote those place cards understood that they should be looked up to.

Klal Yisrael is an *am kohanim* (a nation of priests). To the nations of the world, we represent the spirit of the *Ribono shel Olam*, and what He stands for. They come to us for some holiness. When they see someone who looks the part, whose behavior proclaims his righteousness as he *davens* and gives lots of *tzedakah*, they see a rabbi, even if the person shouldn't technically even be called a "*frum Yid*."

The problem is that we don't want to see ourselves in that light. We want to be just like the next guy. Bernie Green is no different than Albert O'Toole or Mohammed Khafui or Yochanan Schwartzman. We're all capable of doing things that are wrong with our biggest regret being that we got caught.

But that's not how Hashem sees it. To Him, we *are* rabbis. We are teachers, and are meant to be examples for the rest of the world. As Shmuel HaNavi said to Shaul, "If you are small in your own eyes, [realize that] you are the leader of the Tribes of Israel!"

We can't complain if people *call* us rabbis. That shouldn't bother us. What should bother us is if we don't *act* like rabbis — every single one of us. As the Gerrer Rebbe said to the young man who told him, "I learn in Ohr Somayach... b-but I'm NOT a *ba'al teshuvah!*"

Said the Rebbe, "*Nu, fahr vos nisht* (And why not)?"

The Importance of
Being Important

*H*ARDLY A WEEK GOES by when I don't meet someone who hears
my name and says, "Are you the one who writes those articles?" It's a great feeling to know that people enjoy and benefit
from my writing because that's what I'm striving for. One artist
showed me her paintings as a sort of exchange of creativity, and I
thought that was fantastic.

Once I called a fellow for advice with a home do-it-yourself
project I was working on. Now, if you know me, you know that
the phrases "handy" and "Jonathan Gewirtz" hardly exist in the
same universe. Nevertheless, this craftsman offered advice, then
even stopped by to look at my work and explain where I went
wrong, provide the proper part at cost and lend me his tools to do
it. When he got out of his van he said to me, "My wife loves your
articles." There it was! Maybe that's why he was being so nice to
me. Hey, this "being a celebrity" thing is pretty cool. I could get
used to this.

At that time, I meant to write an article about this topic but
as often happens, I forgot and other things came to the fore. But
this past *motzaei Shavuos* something happened which jarred me.
We were saying *kiddush levanah* after *Maariv* and, as is customary, I said "*shalom aleichem*" to three different people who each
responded in turn with the appropriate "*aleichem shalom*."

That's when it hit me. One of the men was a guest in shul for *Yom Tov* and I had not greeted him this way! We went through two days of *davening* together but I only "gave him *shalom*" at the end, when it suited my own needs as part of *kiddush levanah.* How horrible!

Wouldn't he like to feel important? Shouldn't he get the glow of being a "celebrity" when he comes to visit? If we know how good it feels when someone makes us feel important, we should go out of our way to make others feel that way. When you see someone you haven't seen in a while, give him a big hello, hold his hands in yours and flash him a big grin. Tell him how wonderful it is to see him, compliment him on how good he looks or how he brightens up the place with his presence.

If you think you can't do that, that it's not *emes* (truth), know that the complete truth is not necessarily *emes.* The famous difference of opinion relating to how we dance before a bride proves it. Beis Shamai says that at a wedding you praise the bride "as she is." If there's nothing to say, you don't say it. Beis Hillel, on the other hand, whose opinion is the *halachah,* says you praise her as "lovely and graceful." (If you don't believe me, check the song.) *Emes* is saying what Hashem *wants* you to say.

If you tell someone you're happy to see him, over time, you will be. I remember hearing a tape from R' Avigdor Miller *z"l* in which he said, "When you see a Jew, you should bless him! You should think good things and wish him the best." I tried that and sometimes it's amazing what can happen.

I saw a Jewish fellow in the street on my way to work and greeted him with a big "*shalom aleichem.*" Why? Because he was a Jew, a creation of *HaKadosh Baruch Hu,* who had stood shoulder to shoulder with me at *Har Sinai.* He broke out into a big grin. I think I might have made his day. For certain I at least made it brighter.

I was in an out-of-the-way part of Connecticut where I stopped to buy a Powerball lottery ticket. I met a Jew from the other end of the state who knew my father from forty years earlier. If I hadn't gone over to him to greet him, I would never have known and he wouldn't have known that anyone in the store cared he was alive. I didn't win the lottery, but I definitely hit the jackpot.

But you don't have to take my word for it either. It's not my idea. Aharon HaKohen used to go over to people, total sinners, and give them a warm how-do-you-do. They would melt. "How can I sin when Aharon treats me so nicely? If he knew what I have done, he would *never* speak to me with such respect." They would repent and go in the right way, only because someone made them feel like a celebrity.

It's no coincidence that Hillel, whose *beis midrash* was taught to praise the *kallah* no matter what, was also the one who said, "Be from the students of Aharon, who love peace and pursue peace, who love people and bring them closer to Torah." When we show people that they matter, that they are important celebrities to us, they will not only feel better, but will actually become better.

Yeah, I could get used to the celebrity thing. Couldn't you?

Towards Less Picturesque Speech

O NE DAY AT WORK (yes, I do have a day job) a woman was frustrated about something that hadn't worked out as she planned. When she realized what happened, and that she would have to do a whole lot of work over, she let out an exclamation of a slightly vulgar nature. Now, as swear words go, I think most people would consider the severity of what she said to lie somewhere between throwing a gum wrapper out the car window and tearing that tag off the mattress. But when she realized what she said, and that I had heard it, she clapped her hand over her mouth and blushed.

I was ecstatic. Not because she had used foul language of course, or that she had to do the work over, but that when she looked at me, she understood that what she said was not something I would say, or even want to hear. It means that the efforts I take to make a *kiddush Hashem* by not just being the average office worker are bearing fruit.

When I was much younger, perhaps seventeen years old, I remember going to Coulby Park, across the street from our yeshivah, to play softball. One field over was a younger group of kids from the neighborhood, who didn't hide their feelings about the "Jew boys." We tried to ignore them, but what happened next made me pity them tremendously. One boy, perhaps twelve or thirteen, was hit by one of his friends who was taking a practice swing. He let loose a barrage of every word in the book, and a few I think he made up! His tirade of cuss words would have made a pirate blush, and it made me pity him. Here was a kid who for all intents and purposes seemed to be normal, perhaps even intelligent.

Then, in a moment, he turned his mouth into a sewer and showed just how low he could sink. Now, lest you think that I am a prude, who has never used foul language in his life, I wish I could say it was true. But, alas, when I was in seventh grade, in a very far away city, it was *de rigueur* for kids to show how "grown up" they were by spouting off obscenities in normal conversation. It got so bad that they had to bring in the principal to talk to us. They tried to explain to us how bad *nivul peh* (foul language, literally "disgrace of the mouth") was, but I don't think that's what got to me.

Over the years, I have somehow been very fortunate to learn *mussar*, to become more sensitive to others, and to try to sanctify Hashem's name by setting a good example for people who see me going about my daily life. *Baruch Hashem*, I have shunned the company of the "good time Charlies" at work over the years, and never found myself needing to ingratiate myself to them by speaking coarsely or telling off-color jokes.

Now, this is unusual for me because I love humor. I find wordplay electrifying and I like to make people laugh. But there are two types of laughter. One is the kind that happens when someone slips on a banana peel or gets a pie in the face. I never found that humorous because someone was getting hurt or embarrassed. The other laughter, though, is intellectual, and when a story takes an unusual twist or the villain gets one-upped by his victim, it can be classic.

True, there are some jokes which are only funny if vulgarity is used. But who says you have to say them? We hold ourselves to a higher standard, and for good reason.

Our mouths have power. The power of life and death are in the hand of the tongue, say *Chazal*. You can make someone happy or miserable with the turn of a phrase, and you can make yourself a gentleman or a scoundrel the same way. We even have the power to change circumstances by making statements, such as making something permissible forbidden, simply by uttering a vow. A *Kohen* could make someone *tahor* or not with a single word. We use our mouths for *davening* or *divrei Torah*, comforting people and complimenting them.

With such tremendous power in our speech, how could you reduce it to so much garbage by having a potty mouth?

Someone once approached R' Pam *z"l* to ask about a certain swear word which could be rationally called a spiritual location for punishing the wicked after death. He wanted to hear whether or not R' Pam would consider it *nivul peh*. He strode towards the *rosh yeshivah*, but quickly lost his nerve as he approached. When R' Pam asked what he wanted he replied, "Um, *rebbi*, you know how... you know how there are some words which aren't really swear words, I mean, they're just words, but it's not so nice to say them..." and his voice trailed off.

"Oh," said R' Pam with a knowing glance, "you mean like '*fress*' (to eat gluttonously)." Having gotten his answer, he said, "Yes, *rebbi*, that's what I meant, like '*fress*.'"

We have a nobility of character and a glory of spirit which raises us above the animals of the world, even the ones disguised as humans. I know one fellow at work who would walk into the office and within twelve words he had sworn or cursed ten times. It's like he never heard of adjectives! I cringed when he walked in and finally asked someone to say something to him.

When people get upset and yell, or say nasty things, I can't take it. I have developed such an appreciation for kind and noble speech that hearing anything less is offensive. Yes, even a word like *fress* can make me cringe a little. But I'm not here to talk about myself.

I'm here to talk about you and the crown you wear on your

person every moment of every day. If we were to recognize the royalty we are blessed with, we would never sully ourselves with coarse language or worse, *chas v'shalom*. I remember meeting a fellow in the airport once. We struck up a conversation because that day a plane had made an emergency landing when a boy put on his *tefillin* on a plane and the stewardesses and other passengers panicked.

The fellow was wearing clothing that led me to expect that he valued his *Yiddishkeit* very much. His wife, too, clearly wore clothing reminiscent of an earlier time on a different continent. At one point, in order to emphasize his disbelief of the authorities who grounded the plane, he exclaimed that it was baloney. But he didn't say baloney. Instead, he used a different word that made me cringe. I can't stand to hear such things from *goyim*, why do I have to hear it from the holy mouth of a Jew? He probably thought he was "with it," but I felt bad he didn't realize what he was giving up.

So the next time you have a great joke or story to tell someone, imagine R' Pam is listening intently, with a hopeful smile upon his face. Do you think he'll appreciate the punch line or delivery? If not, do yourself a favor, and remember that words are the accessories of your soul, and a holy Jew like you should dress the part.

Dark Side of the Moon

RECENTLY I EXPERIENCED ANOTHER parking lot incident. I was on my way to *daven Maariv*, and as I was parking my car, I noticed that I was too far back (the lines were too faint to see) and I was taking up two spots. I moved forward and shut off the car. As I got out, I noticed a fellow who was also too far back. However, because he was also at an angle, instead of two spots, he managed to take up three! Not wanting to insult him, I joked, "You're lucky it's not busy right now, I think you took up three spots." I figured he would get back in the car and correct his error. But I was wrong.

Instead, he said, "That should be the worst of my *aveiros* (sins)." I was shocked.

Here was a man on his way to *daven* to Hashem, to ask for what he needed, yet he was willing to knowingly ignore the needs of others and on top of that he was cavalier about the whole thing! It didn't bother him that he was doing something wrong, because he felt it wasn't a big deal. Most likely, he felt he had done much worse.

It's not the first time I've heard this either. I once said to someone, "What if you were in an accident and broke 200 bones. Would you let someone break a few more?"

"At that point you're a cripple anyway," came the response. "What difference does it make?"

Hmm... I don't know, how about more excruciating pain and

236

even more rehab necessary? Why would you knowingly let some-one break another bone?!

Well, I'd like to point out that it very well does make a differ-ence, and I will try to put it in terms you can understand. Imagine you were on your way to pay your mortgage, and you had $1500 in your pocket. When you get to the bank, you find that there was a hole in your pocket and $1100 fell out. Do you: (A) pay the $400 you have and then try to figure out how to replace the rest, or (B) get so angry that you tear up the remaining hundred-dollar bills?

How about this? You notice one of the hundreds that fell out of your pocket sitting on the floor. Do you bother to bend down or just let it lie there until the wind or someone else takes it away?

Now let me ask you, you already lost some and don't have enough to pay the mortgage. What difference does it make if you lose the rest? Clearly, the smaller amount you have left is still very valuable!

But when it comes to *sechar v'onesh* (reward and punishment), people don't see it that way. "I'm going to burn anyway," they say flippantly. Or, "It's okay, I'm already gonna be set to extra crispy." It's amazing that we can joke about things that way, but we do.

Dieters experience the same phenomenon. "I already broke my diet by eating three cookies. I might as well eat the whole bag." But that logic is flawed. If it takes thirty-five minutes on the treadmill to burn off the three cookies, what will it take for the other twenty-seven? (It's a rhetorical question, no need to do the math, but it's ten times longer than it would have taken [ok, nine times.])

We know that it makes no sense to throw in the towel, to give up and say it doesn't make a difference. Logically speaking, if there is a reward for each positive action and a punishment for each negative action (and they don't offset, by the way. Hashem pun-ishes for all the bad stuff, so you can enjoy the full reward of the mitzvos later), why do we assume it doesn't make a difference?

The answer is that it isn't our rational brains telling us it doesn't matter. It's one of the oldest tricks in the *yetzer hara*'s playbook. Saying "It's too late," or "I'm too far gone," is a way for people to cop out and give up. But guess what? It *does* make a difference.

Each month, we say *kiddush levanah* and we praise and *daven* to Hashem about the moon. Do we do it when it's at its fullest? Nope. We say this prayer at the beginning of the month, when it's just beginning to be visible. In other words, we look for the light of the moon when most of it is in shadow.

Instead of saying, "It's mostly dark, what's the point?" we appreciate and strain to see that sliver of light which signals a return to greatness and the glorious full moon. As long as there's a little light, we focus on that and thank Hashem, asking that he return the moon to its former glory.

Klal Yisrael is compared to the moon. We may have faltered, we may have erred. But if we can find the bits of light within us and appreciate them, we can rise again. So the guy who took up three spots, or the person speaking *lashon hara*, or the person who finds much of Judaism archaic, should recognize that by being considerate of the others and reparking, or stopping themselves even at the end of a long gossip session from saying that one last story, or finding the joy in the mitzvos and realizing that there is much meaning in all we do, they can actually make a huge difference.

They can light up the world and themselves like the moon, which despite falling into shadow again and again, always returns to cast its heavenly glow on us all.

What Makes a Kiddush Hashem

O NE DAY, I HAD a return to do at Wal-Mart. I know what you're thinking: this is going to be an article about *yissurim shel ahavah* and suffering with purpose. But no, that's not this week's topic.

I entered the store and went to the returns line. As I did, I noticed a store employee struggling with a lawn swing a customer was buying. He was trying to get it out the door on a large cart and she was nervously watching him with arms folded.

As he attempted to wheel it out the door, the swing's large box banged the top and he realized it could not get out while on the cart. Very conscious of my yarmulke and *tzitzis* (not to mention my beard and overall very Jewish appearance) I put down my box, receipt on top, and ran to help. I told him to carry the box outside while I wheeled the cart. As he passed through the first door, we realized the second door would present the same problem so I ended up walking him outside and helping him get the box onto the cart before heading back to my return in the line.

What greeted me was rather overwhelming. "I watched your box!" said one woman waiting in line. "And I saved your place!" chimed in another. They were so thrilled to be part of my thoughtfulness. "Nobody ever helps anymore," said the woman who had watched the box, to her daughter. "Nobody tries to lend a hand." Now, if this woman had wanted to teach her daughter a better lesson, she could have helped him with the cart, but thankfully,

I got the mitzvah and the opportunity to show these people what being a Jew is about.

The line happened to be moving very quickly, and the woman ahead of me made a pleasant comment about it. I spoke up and said to the cashier, "We're talking about you!" She grimaced and was ready for the worst. I continued, "We were just saying what a good job you were doing to get us all taken care of as quickly as possible." The other people in line voiced their agreement and the clerk broke out in a huge grin. "You just made my day!" Chalk up another *kiddush Hashem* for the man in beard and yarmulke.

Truly, making a *kiddush Hashem* is easier than you might think, and the rewards are beyond understanding. We know how severe the sin of *chillul Hashem* is, *chas v'shalom*, that even *teshuvah* can't fix it and a person needs the *kaparah* of death, so imagine how great the reward for *kiddush Hashem* is. Not only that, Hashem's reward for good is 500 times the punishment for bad so even the smallest *kiddush Hashem* is a huge opportunity.

I know of one fellow who was given what might have been incorrect change. Not only did he say something, but he first exited the store and waited a few minutes to make sure that when he came back, it would be noticeable. They commented on how wonderful it was that this Orthodox Jew bothered himself to come back for a few pennies. A few pennies here, untold riches in *Gan Eden*!

Now, you may be thinking that these are the ultimate types of *kiddush Hashem*, showing the non-Jews around us what God's chosen people are made of. But you'd be wrong. It's a much bigger *kiddush Hashem* to do what's right in front of Jews, in order to remind ourselves what we are made of, what is expected of us, and what we are capable of doing.

In fact, if we are not doing what others want us to do because it would be contrary to the Torah, that is a true *kiddush Hashem*, even if we think people will look down on us. There is no mitzvah to make peace at the expense of the Torah, and *kiddush Hashem* is not about being "a nice guy."

But there is a much bigger *kiddush Hashem* that I was *zocheh* to witness. I was standing outside the kosher supermarket talking to a friend; let's call him "David" (*his real name is Hershel*).

So Hershel and I were talking and I pointed out a shopping cart sitting in the middle of the parking lot. A woman was carrying things from her car into a store and walked right past it without even pushing it downhill with her foot. She walked back to get more items, and, despite empty hands, didn't spare a second to move the cart. This happened a few times and then Hershel raced me to go move it (he won).

As we continued our conversation, we saw a fellow leaving the store with two small children in tow. This fellow was known to both of us as a pious man involved in *harbatzas Torah* (but that's a whole 'nother "Shmuz"). We wondered what he would do.

Hershel didn't have time to wait around but I really wanted to see what this man would do. I saw him unload his groceries, put the children in the car, and then walk the shopping cart over to the cart return aisle. He could have been excused from returning it perhaps, encumbered as he was with the two children, and with his spot so far from the store. Of course, he didn't know I was watching so that wasn't a factor.

I thought he might just put it up on the curb which would show he was thoughtful and considerate of others, but he did more, and put it where it belonged. He did what was right because that's what Hashem wants from us, and he showed me what Jews are made of. I was moved. I drove over from where I had been watching the scene unfold and said to him, "I want you to know, you just made a tremendous *kiddush Hashem* — on me."

A few days later, I was at another store and saw a shopping cart in the middle of a space, two spots from the cart return aisle! (That's like eighteen feet; people walk farther to get socks from their drawer.) I was incensed. I saw a few *bachurim* unloading their groceries into a nearby car and called out to them. "Do you see this?!" I exclaimed. "This is just *rishus* (wickedness)!" I moved the cart just in time for a woman to pull in and take the spot, something the previous shopper didn't care if she did or not.

"It's a *chillul Hashem*," replied one of the boys. "Our Rosh Yeshivah just spoke about that." I realized he was exactly right. I was surprised in the negative sense by what Jews are capable of. (Yes, I know that cart might have been left by the one non-Jew who shopped at the store amongst the hundreds of Jews, but I've witnessed too many Jewish people doing the same to assume that none are ever insensitive.)

The woman thanked me when she realized what I had done, and thanked me for my articles (I guess my cover was blown) and walked into the store. As I reflected on it, I realized that I had just made a *kiddush Hashem* in place of a bad situation, and how much we owe to the people who, like the father of two at the end of the parking lot, constantly inspire us with their own *kiddush Hashem*.

Now You're Talking

FOR YEARS, PEOPLE HAVE been quoting an apocryphal statistic that people's number one fear is public speaking, followed by heights and spiders, with death a distant seventh. In the words of R' Yeruchem Seinfeld, that means that at a funeral, most people would rather be in the *aron* than giving the *hesped*.

I can't say that it's true, but as a speechwriter, I do know that some people are terrified about the prospect, and that's why it's important to have well-thought-out remarks. That way, you know you won't say anything to embarrass yourself.

That's also why I find it so surprising how people will say things in public (just not onstage) without the words having actually crossed their frontal lobes, and missing the medulla oblongata by a mile. They have no qualms about making ridiculous, embarrassing remarks, and thinking that they're witty at the same time.

I often listen to *shiurim* while I drive and once I was listening to a *shiur*-on-cassette from a tape library. I usually let it run to the end so it's rewound for the next person (I can still be kind and rewind.) At the end of the *shiur*, the speaker mentioned that the following week we would change the clock so the *shiur* would begin at 10:30. Some wiseguy called out from the audience, "Rabbi, we aren't changing the clocks, we keep the same ones."

As the tape made its way to the end I heard people coming up and asking questions. After a few minutes of questions and answers at the lectern, I heard a familiar voice, only louder this time. "Rabbi," he said with obvious pride at his brilliance, "you said we're changing the clocks. We aren't changing them, we're keeping the same ones!" The speaker gave a half-hearted laugh, trying to humor the fellow, and the tape ended. But not for me.

I couldn't stop thinking about how this fellow had stood there for five or six minutes to make this embarrassingly ridiculous comment. And he thought he was smart! Here he was, public speaking without even realizing it. Maybe if he knew that he was being taped for people to hear years later he would have gotten some of the well-touted fear and kept his mouth shut. One would think that at some point in his standing there waiting, the thought would have crossed his mind that it was a silly joke, and he would be wasting the speaker's time. Now, in his defense, he didn't say anything wrong, just kind of lame.

Another time, I was at a *minyan* when the rabbi mentioned a new restaurant in town. "There's no new restaurant," called out one man with a snicker, "the frozen pizza I put in my oven tastes better than the frozen pizza they put in theirs! I wouldn't call that a restaurant." So he got to make his public-speaking debut with a negative comment, which violated about half-a-dozen laws of *lashon hara*, and guess what? He thought he was smart! And I'm sure he never imagined just how far his words would travel, to all of you reading this today.

The Ramban in his famous letter advises, "Think about the words before you speak them from your mouth." One reason is that once you speak, your words go out into the world and you have no more control over them. Another is that they can have a powerful effect on listeners, so why would you waste them?

When I was in yeshivah, a friend got married and three of us were invited to Shabbos *sheva berachos*. As we were the *chasan*'s friends, we were invited to speak by the meals. The other two fellows spoke Friday night, and included primarily jokes, with a *chasan Torah vort* thrown in for balance. (In his defense, the second fellow tried to include more Torah. He also might be reading this…)

When my turn came Shabbos morning, they were expecting me, always known as a joker, to deliver more of the same. I instead offered an intriguing approach to the *berachah* "*Mazel Tov*," in light of the Gemara's (*Shabbos* 156) discussion of *ein mazel l'Yisrael*, and followed it up with an inspirational pep-talk based on "*hachodesh hazeh lachem*," tying it in not only to the *chasan*, but to everyone listening. They were spellbound.

I had gotten up and offered a serious speech which was entertaining at the same time. People remembered what I said afterwards instead of just that I had gotten up and made some wisecracks to fill time. Often, people approach a speech thinking their primary focus is entertainment. That's far from the truth. Words are very powerful and should be weighed before use.

In 1938, a young man gave a *Shabbos Shuvah derashah* at the Young Israel of Eastern Parkway. A woman came over to him afterwards and said, "Rabbi, we have been having a lecture series here for some time, but I learned more in your forty-five minutes than I did in all the hours of lectures I sat through before."

When he came back to his *rebbi*, R' Dovid Leibowitz *z"l* (great-nephew of the Chafetz Chaim and founder of the yeshivah that bears his name, older *chavrusa* of R' Yaakov Kamenetzky *z"l* and father of R' Henoch Leibowitz *z"l*), he told him what he had said in his *derashah*.

R' Dovid asked him, "In what language did you speak?" Somewhat ashamed, the fellow admitted he had spoken in English, not *Yiddish*.

"*Oy!*" exclaimed R' Dovid as he clapped his hands together, "If only I could speak English well enough to be able to reach the people. I could revolutionize America!" That is the purpose of speech — to reach people, and help them to reach as well. That young man was my grandfather, R' Abba Zalka Gewirtz *z"l*, and *baruch Hashem* I have inherited the gravity of that message from him. Now, I'm passing it along.

So, the next time you have a great zinger to say, or a "hysterically funny" cynical comment, or you have the opportunity to do some public speaking, think carefully about what you're going to say.

Remember, your words will be recorded for posterity — on the hearts and souls of your listeners.

Thoughts from All Over

ALTHOUGH I HAVE TRIED in this book to put things into categories, sometimes you simply can't. As you've likely recognized by now, inspiration can be had anywhere, anytime, and by anyone.

The items in this last section are a compilation of thoughts, musings, and articles that didn't necessarily fit into a category of their own. Rather, these are meaningful messages, suitable for all occasions, that just had to be mentioned before we go.

Caught in the Act

ARLY ONE FRIDAY MORNING, I went grocery shopping. (Monsey is a lovely, serene, place at 8 A.M.) As I went to park, it was clear that the fellow whose job it was to return the shopping carts had not gotten to do his work yet. I skillfully slid into a spot from which I could walk to the door, passing two shopping carts left blocking good parking spots, and grabbed them both. As I began walking them to the door, a woman pointed her finger at me.

"I know who you are," she said in an almost accusatory tone, "and why you're doing that." Yes, I had been spotted as The Observant Jew. I asked how she knew who I was and she responded, "I read all your articles and love them" (I believe that's how the conversation went, I could just be imagining it…), "and I know your wife."

Okay, so maybe my actions weren't entirely how she knew me, but I sure am glad that she caught me returning shopping carts and not doing something embarrassing or worse! That would be awful, to be doing something I'm not proud of and have someone say, "Hey, I know you!"

While we're on the topic of grocery shopping, let's flash forward to a day when I had run to the gym, and was rushing to pick up my daughter from an after-school program. There I was, decked out in my finest gym clothes and baseball cap, standing at the supermarket fidgeting while trying to figure out which line might be the shortest.

A woman in the line saw me standing there and offered to let me go ahead of her. I really appreciated it and told her as much. "Well," she said, "I guess this will be my mitzvah for the day."

"I bet you do many mitzvos you're not even aware of," I told her. "*Chazal* tell us that 'even the emptiest of [*Klal Yisrael*] are as full of mitzvos as a pomegranate [is full of seeds.]' When you open a pomegranate and take out the seeds, you may think there are no more. Then you pull back another layer and voilà, there are a whole bunch you didn't know were there. That's what every Jew is like." On top of that, I was impressed that she had noticed that I looked like I was in a hurry. She was sensitive to others, yet she was content to think her only mitzvah was letting me go first.

As we waited for the woman ahead of us to open her purse, dig out exact change, in dollars and cents, and slowly put it on the counter coin by coin (which my benefactor commented she would never do when people were waiting), she noticed another fellow in line with only two items and let him go before her as well. This was a moment in her life, one brief episode, that lay bare before others what she was capable of. I hope she reads this and recognizes the gravity of her actions. To her, it was nothing special. To those watching her, it was a defining moment.

I once heard that the Rambam writes that whatever you are doing at the last moment of your life is what you remain doing for all eternity. That's a scary thought. Imagine someone who gets so upset about something that he blows up and starts yelling at the top of his lungs. He has a heart attack and dies. Would he want to be in that state for five hundred thousand years? Or longer?!

Or if his time was up when he was in the middle of looking at something he shouldn't be. Yes, the people who found him would all know what he had done, but worse, for all time, he would be in a constant state of sinning.

Living a Torah life isn't made up of what happened yesterday, but what's happening now; every moment. Do you live as a Jew?

Think as a Jew? Would you be proud to have whatever you're do-ing right now captured for posterity? Because it is. Every moment we're alive, we're caught in the act.

There's an eye that sees, an ear that hears, and a camera that shoots in HD, 3D and any other D you can think of. Maybe we just call it God? All we do is being recorded, and at any given moment, the spotlight can be cast upon us. That's a sobering thought, but one that will do us a lot of good to keep in mind.

Imagine you were in a big contest, just you didn't know it. You were subjected to grueling tests, annoying people, and difficult situations. Finally, when you think you can't take it anymore, the cameraman steps forward and they tell you that you were being broadcast around the world to video billboards in every major city. The world had been watching your every move and saw your grace under pressure. You win a big prize.

Now think what would have been if you had blown your top and would be remembered forever for that outburst. This could be a very motivational meditation to live each moment as if it was your last; as if it would define you for all time. Because, by the way, it does.

My Daddy Is a Fix-It Man

I'M NOT SURE WHAT precipitated this comment from my three-year-old, but it was humorous and heartwarming at the same time. I'm not known as the handiest of fellows, or as my wife puts it, "my talents lie elsewhere." While I may be able to write a speech that will knock people's socks off, I couldn't build a drawer to put them in.

Anyway, I may have put the head of my daughter's doll back on, or taped a torn sheet of paper together, but when she said, "My Daddy is a fix-it man!" with such pure and simple faith that her father could do anything, I felt like a superman. I actually felt like I could fix anything, and, fortunately, I have pretty good health insurance coverage, but that's another story...

It was a phenomenal feeling, but let's face it: I am the kind of guy who thinks a Phillip's screwdriver is something you drink when you have an upset stomach and a nail gun is a faster alternative to a nail clipper. So is she wrong? Can I possibly be a fix-it man?

In *Chazal*, we find an expression that someone is a *chaver* (one of us). He knows what's what and is regarded highly. So what defines a *chaver*? The Gemara in several places says that a *chaver* "will not let something go from his hand unless he has fixed it." For example, if he dies, we assume he tithed his fruits even if they were picked that day because he does not let things sit in a state where others might err. When he gets the chance to fix something, he does it.

In other words, he is a "fix-it man."

I remember in yeshivah once when I was taking care of something or other and wanted to get it done right. One *kollel* fellow commented to a former *rebbi* of mine that I was a chaver, not letting things go without taking care of them. I think one of them then made a comment about finding me an *eishes chaver*, but I digress.

I don't think I understood the depth of that compliment at that tender age, but I can honestly say that now, I imagine that to be a very big vote of confidence. I think it's one we could all stand to hear once in a while, and it's what was embodied in my little girl's lovingly proud statement, "My Daddy is a fix-it man."

So, how can any of us get that wonderful feeling? By trying to become "fix-it" men and women. Think about it. You know an older boy or girl looking for a *shidduch*. Do you have them in mind? R' Paysach Krohn did, and came up with special *shidduch* cards for people to carry with them and be able to more easily interact with others.

When you hear that someone lost his job, do you say, "*Oy*," or do you call him to offer support, or better yet, try to find him a job? If someone is ill, do you shake your head, or reach for a *Tehillim*? R' Akiva famously freshened up the room of an ill student, opening the windows and making his bed more comfortable. His student immediately felt better and said, "*Rebbi*, you saved my life." He didn't just feel bad his student was sick, nor did he "fulfill the mitzvah of visiting the sick." He did what he could to make things better.

It doesn't have to be a big thing. Putting a shopping cart back where it belongs is one thing you can do to restore order to the world. [Sorry, I'm under contract to mention them at least once a month, barring unforeseen circumstances.]

It could be putting your *sefer* back on the shelf so the next person looking for it doesn't waste ten minutes, or holding your packages so the seat next to you on the bus is available for someone else. Perhaps, it's doing something to make sure you or the people around you don't speak *lashon hara*, a HUGE *tikun* for both those involved and the whole world. (For simple, practical *lashon hara* prevention, check out segulah4singles.com.)

The point is that you should want to make things right. It's not just because I'm saying so, but because we are supposed to emulate *HaKadosh Baruch Hu* and HE'S a fix-it man (or Being — sorry, no word is just right).

How do I know? Because three times a day we *daven* and say Hashem is "*Gomel chasadim tovim, v'koneh hakol,*" this means that he grants us good kindnesses and is "*koneh*" everything. Some people translate that to mean He "acquires everything" or "takes ownership." Others say it comes from the root of "*tikun*" or "*mesaken,*" meaning to fix up, as found, for example, relating to a *chaver*, who takes ownership of things and doesn't let them go until he fixes them. Don't you see? Our Heavenly Daddy is a fix-it man too!

If we want emulate Hashem, a great way to do it is to do good kindnesses for others, and work to make things right. And best of all, there's nothing like feeling you can achieve anything you put your mind to. So go ahead, get out your tool belt, fire up the pneumatic drill, grab a few Band-aids, and put up a big sign that says, "I am a fix-it man!"

All I Need To Know I Learned From My Kindergartner

THERE IS A COMMON understanding that with age comes wisdom. I'd like to agree and challenge that at the same time. I think as we approach "the Golden Years" we achieve a certain amount of wisdom through life experience, and this is why one must stand up for anyone who is over seventy years of age. However, I think that at a certain level, we become stupider as we get older. Now, before you start disagreeing, or telling me that there is no such word as stupider, let me explain.

Any parent will happily regale you with tales of their child's brilliance. How at only two, he could say, "gapa," which you knew meant "I want to go to the park for, oh, how I love the swings and monkey bars" and how your daughter immediately knew something was wrong when the gum she found on the sidewalk didn't taste right. But do we really think they're so smart? I wonder.

Let me give you an example. This is a true story that really happened. Two boys, let's call them Yosef and Noach, were friends, on different teams in *Pirchei* baseball. When they found out they were to play against each other in the same game, each was so excited to be able to play with his friend. In his innocent exuberance, Yosef said, "Oh boy! I can't wait. I hope Noach wins!" Now, the adults around will give this story a grin, sympathetically clucking at the innocent notion of the boy who didn't realize that if his friend Noach

255

were to win, his own team would lose. He missed the point of the game, which is that your team is supposed to win, not the other's.

Another example: Friends gave my two-year-old daughter a present. Before she even opened the present, she danced wildly around in circles with it, exuding pure elation. "Daddy!" she cried, as she pointed to the "My Little Pony" wrapping paper, "I got ponies!" As a father, I smiled at her naïveté, as if to say, "Silly girl, the paper isn't the gift; it's what's inside the paper that's important."

Now, let's look at these stories and decide who is really making the mistake. In the first case, the boy was so happy for his friend and wished him well. That is the ultimate expression of good sportsmanship, and better yet, of *middos tovos*. He could have looked at the grown-ups and said, "You think playing is about winning? It's about feeling good and enjoying yourself. If I feel good and am happy when my friend wins, haven't I progressed beyond your simple understanding of the point?" If we think about it, the child has just exhibited the maturity we would attribute to someone much more advanced in years and with tremendous life experience. We would understand if someone with white hair (whatever was left of it) would say, "I don't care about winning, it means more to someone else," but if we hear it from a six-year-old we think it's a mistake.

What about the girl who was over the moon about the wrapping paper? Could she not have turned to me and said, "But Daddy, if you appreciate even the little things, such as the paper that a gift is wrapped in, and find the joy in them, won't you be able to appreciate the gift inside that much more?"

How truly wise she is beyond her years. But it is not the wisdom of experience; I believe it is the wisdom of a pure soul, as yet uncorrupted by the materialistic world around us.

The Chovos HaLevavos, in his brilliant, enlightening discussion on humility, lists the benefits of being humble enjoyed both in this world and the next. The first benefit of being humble, he says, is that you are happy with your lot. You don't expect anything, so you appreciate every bit of Hashem's kindness. In addition, you are better able to cope with life's challenges because you don't feel you "deserve" better (now THERE'S a dangerous phrase), and you can calmly do what you need to do.

What does it mean that you are able to enjoy every little detail? It means that you are happy to get the ponies on your wrapping paper, even if you don't really like the gift; that you take pleasure in seeing the joy on your friend's face when he accomplishes, even if you have to lose for it to happen; that you are able to ignore the mess your child made in the kitchen and appreciate the gooey cupcake she prepared for you.

It means that you can come closer to that pure state of the *neshamah* which recognizes the kindness of the Almighty. That you can rise above the pettiness and regain the charm of the innocent children.

Let me leave you with one last story to illustrate my point. One winter, our family traveled to Florida for vacation during winter break from school. When my daughter returned to nursery school, each child was asked to name something they did over the break. My daughter responded, "I saw my Bobbie and Zeidy, and rode on a train."

When we heard what she had said, my wife looked at me quizzically. "We flew down to Florida. What is she saying about a train ride?" It took me a minute, but then it clicked. "Remember when we came back from the airport? We took a monorail to the long-term parking lot. That was her 'train ride.'"

So, my three-year-old was able to find the same joy and appreciation she had from seeing her grandparents in something as simple and mundane as a four-minute train ride. We saw it as a burden, another obstacle to overcome, but she saw it as an adventure, a gift. Children are very wise; we would be wise to learn from them.

The Apple of My "i"

*H*AVE YOU NOTICED LATELY the overwhelming plethora of items whose names begin with an "i"? Now, I don't mean ice cream or invisible ink. I mean things like iPod, iTunes, iHome, iTuna Fish Sandwich and so on. It's kind of driving me crazy because things which have no connection to iPods are getting that little prefix as if they are part of some sort of digital revolution. In fact, some people are calling today's teens the iGeneration. But what's it all about, Apple?

Well, back when Apple Computer introduced one of its new computers, the big selling point was that it could get set up and onto the internet in just a few minutes. To symbolize that, they named it iMac. The "i" was short for internet.

When they came out with their music players, they kept that stylization and called it the iPod, presumably because someone envisioned iTunes, where you would buy music off the internet. Since both of these were tremendous successes, it spawned a huge copycat craze. At first, companies that made accessories for the iPod used iNames to identify their products but now it's just totally out of hand.

To be perfectly honest, I think one reason it annoys me so much is that besides the cutesy-ness of it, it gives Apple a certain superhuman quality which plays up to the seeming arrogance of those superior-minded Apple folks. Anyone who has a Mac will tell you how the PC is a joke and the Mac is great, and usually they will add how sad it is for you who "don't get it." I for one can do without the whole übercomputer attitude.

However, I must say that I recently learned a thing or two about that company which made me rethink my stance — well, at least a little. One Shabbos, a young couple came to lunch at our home. I asked the woman what she did, and she said, "I work for Apple."

Jokingly, but with a really good straight face, I said, "So you sell iPods?"

"Well, yes," she replied, completely serious, "and computers, and other Apple products."

I was rather taken aback until her husband explained that she was getting her degree in Computer Science but Apple has a rule that if you want to have any job in the company, you have to start in retail. Why? Presumably so you can get a better understanding of whom you're designing products for and what people want when they purchase electronics.

After some time in retail, people get promoted to various departments, including Research and Development, Programming, Public Relations, etc.

Now, I must admit, this is thinking out of the iBox. Years ago, I learned about the psychological defense mechanism of "projection." (Thanks Rabbi Brog!) In it, one attributes to others his own fears or negative thoughts. In other words, the individual perceives in others the motive he denies having himself. Thus the cheat is sure that everyone else is dishonest.

Now, in a non-clinical sense, I think we project all the time without it being a defense mechanism. How many times have we said, "It's like a sauna in here!" only to find out it's 71°F and others are comfortable but we've broken out in a sweat? It's like having to put on a sweater because your mother is cold. If we find some music too loud, we assume everyone else does too.

Now let's apply this to business. When something appeals to

us, we assume it will appeal to others as well. We offer products we would want, at the prices we think fair, in a manner we would listen to, and wonder why it doesn't work.

Guess what? People are different and see things differently. If we only have the prism of our own views through which to look at the world, we will never be able to see things as others do. This is what *Chazal* meant by, "*Al tadin es chaveiro ad shetavo li'mkomo* — Don't judge your friend until you've come to his place." If you can't see why your friend did something, maybe that's because you don't think like he does or see things as he does.

If someone said something you consider thoughtless, or did something that was obviously rude, maybe it's only obvious to you and they had a different outlook on it?

That's why I must take a step back and appreciate what Apple is doing. They're focusing on the customer, the end user, someone else. The ego no longer rules, the "I" is willing to listen to what someone else wants, and humble itself before another. Instead of I, it's now i. A softer, gentler self.

Wouldn't it be great if we could all become "i"s, able to take our minds off ourselves for a minute and listen, really listen, to others? That would be completely revolutionary.

The Tefillin Connection

*H*ELLO AGAIN EVERYONE, and welcome to another segment of, "Jews in the News." This week, we will not discuss a "religious" person who committed a crime, nor a "philanthropic Jew" who was found to be a swindler. We won't even discuss a bearded ultra-Orthodox Jew whose actions were shown to be in direct contradiction to his religious "principles." No, these are the stories the world would like you to hear, but which cause us much sorrow, along with the *chillul Hashem* caused within our own folds.

Today, however, we will hear of a *kiddush Hashem*. Now, some people will likely find a way to cast aspersions on the protagonist of our story, but I believe this item became newsworthy for a special reason.

A while ago, a young man boarded an early morning flight at La Guardia airport and, as it was just after sunrise, he *davened* on the plane. There was some confusion about his *tefillin* possibly being a bomb and the plane made an emergency landing. Twenty minutes later, the frightened boy was released.

Now, people are taking sides over whether he was right or wrong, whether he should have assumed that people would think his *tefillin* were a bomb, but I know I have seen crazier things on a plane that didn't arouse suspicion. Be that as it may, I strongly believe that this story made headlines because the *Ribono shel Olam* wanted us to get a message. Whatever the reason, the boy didn't think he shouldn't put on his *tefillin*, and the events unfolded as they did.

First of all, according to the Rambam, doing a mitzvah, despite it getting funny looks from people, is a *kiddush Hashem*, not a *chillul Hashem*. Here was someone who caused a great *kiddush Hashem* (which primarily is supposed to be geared towards Jews, not Gentiles) by making us think about *tefillin*. Second of all, perhaps this was the very reason Hashem chose for this to happen to a young man, who can be excused for not thinking along terror lines.

It is no coincidence that this happened on Thursday of *Parshas Bo*, in which we find two of the four *parshiyos* in the *tefillin*! Not only that, but these *parshiyos* relate to how we live in this world, and how we behave based on our obligations to Hashem for taking us out of Egypt.

I was told that some people posting on various "Jewish news" websites attributed the hoopla to the *pasuk* in *Va'Eschanan*, that "The nations of the land will see that Hashem's Name is called upon you and fear you," which *Chazal* say refers to *tefillin shel Rosh*.

According to them, this was an example of *tefillin* striking fear into the nations. To those people I say, with the utmost respect, "Phooey!" I think it was exactly the opposite.

The Torah does not say the nations will be frightened when we wear *tefillin*. *Tefillin* are not some sort of weapon or threat to them. Rather, the Torah says they will see Hashem's name upon us, meaning that they will look at us and say, "This is one who does the bidding of Hashem. He wears the uniform of Hashem by his actions conforming to God's clearly defined guidance." Then they will be in awe and have reverence for us.

The fact that they saw the *tefillin* not as an object with which we commune with our Creator, or fulfill His mitzvos, but rather as a weapon, an object of destruction, reflects poorly on us. Perhaps, it is *we* who don't see *tefillin* for what they really are.

If we saw *tefillin* as catalysts to ensuring that our actions and thoughts are holy as befitting the nation of *HaKadosh Baruch Hu*, then the world would see them the same way. If, however, we see them, and perhaps many other mitzvos, as merely a routine we must go through because we want to do what God wants, why should the world see them as something special?

His story hit home especially hard because something happened to me for the first time I can remember. That same day, I traveled from La Guardia (and I also don't remember the last time I flew from there) but unlike that boy, I forgot my *tefillin*. I didn't realize until the next morning. I managed to borrow a pair where I was staying, but my mother-in-law (*der shvigger leiben*) drove from Brooklyn to Monsey to get my *tefillin* and bring them to me when she came to join us two days later.

"I know that there's something special between men and their *tefillin*," she said. "I know it's not the same if you don't have your own." It struck me. I didn't feel that way. I was happy to have any pair to fulfill the mitzvah, but that made me sad. Why didn't I have a *kesher* to my *tefillin*?

Here was something that bound me to Hashem, traveled with me from the time I was thirteen years old and helped me fulfill a mitzvah every day, and yet I didn't feel connected! How could I be so cavalier about my *tefillin*? When I put on the borrowed *tefillin* that day, I noted that they didn't fit the same way.

My *tefillin* seem to know exactly where to lay and how to wrap around my arm. They suit me perfectly. How many other mitzvos does Hashem orchestrate to fit us exactly? What about our spouses, offering us opportunities to come closer to the *Ribono shel Olam* all the time? Do we acknowledge how perfect they are for us, or do we merely accept them as just one more responsibility?

Are there people in our lives whom we think we could do without? If they're there, it's because Hashem knows we need them to be. But somehow we miss that. Until now.

When something like this happens, it makes us stop and think.

Tsunamis and earthquakes shake up the world, but we shouldn't get as excited by physical manifestations of Divine providence as we do by the more miraculous and spiritual ones. Here's a case where Hashem is reminding us of His presence.

On the week when the Torah talks about *tefillin* creating a special bond between us and our God, representing eternal life, the world makes the mistake in thinking that this same item could be a tool of death. It's not a coincidence; it's a wakeup call.

The boy's grandmother was quoted as saying, "Perhaps something good will come of it." If even one person reading this article takes more notice of the kindnesses of Hashem, or looks at *tefillin* or other things with a greater sense of appreciation and reverence, then something good will have come of it — we will have gotten the message.

There's a Sucker Born
Every Minute

F OR YEARS, MY FATHER was the rabbi of the shul. We moved
around and wherever we went, I was "the rabbi's son." Rather
austere monikers for both of us it seems to me. At one point, we
moved and my father began to lead a smaller *minyan*. At that time,
he took on another role with a tantalizing, almost magical sound:
Candy Man. The point of the Candy Man is to train kids to equate
shul with sweetness, much as when a young child licks honey off
the letters of the *alef-beis* on his first day of school. When they get
older, hopefully they will be attracted by the sweet opportunity of
communicating with Hashem, instead of the short-term physical
gratification of *Kiddush* club or a good shmooze.

Anyway, at his *minyan*, my father took the initiative to start
giving out candies, lollipops, and whatever else he or my mother
came up with. My wife remembers coming to shul as a *kallah* and
finding a *siddur* and lollipop waiting for her. Fast forward ten years
to when she realized that the shul I was *davening* in didn't have
a Candy Man and she suggested I grab the opportunity. Unlike
some shuls which have elections and campaign signs for this lofty
position, for me, all it took was a big Ziploc bag full of lollies.

Now, it has been rough sometimes, making sure I didn't forget
to buy more, rummaging through my kids' school snacks when I
did forget, and *chas v'shalom* not leaving the bag with just yellow

lollies left. But it has also been very enlightening and I wish to share my observations with you.

In my experiences, I have come across several distinct behavior patterns when it comes to children and the Candy Man. I think that many of these traits stay with the children because I have witnessed the same attitudes in plenty of adults. Now, while children will have different ways of going about it, getting a candy from the Candy Man (or Lollyman, if you prefer) has almost universal appeal. If we say, "*Chanoch la'naar al pi darko*, train the child according to his natural tendencies," could it be that going to the Candy Man is the great equalizer of primary education in life?

The Behavioral Patterns

1. **The Instinctive Sucker:** This child is utterly focused on his candy. He sees his prize and knows what he wants. He doesn't think about where it comes from so he needs his father to remind him to say thank you.

   This is an interesting case, because if his father never got past this stage, he is only focused on his kid getting a lolly, and maybe behaving for five minutes, and may not think about making him say thank you.

2. **The Payoff:** This is the kid who knows how to work the system. He runs over, grabs a lolly and mumbles "thanks" as he whizzes back to play with his friends. Of course you have to say thank you, but who says you have to mean it? His expression of gratitude falls a little flat but because he's a kid, you let it go. When he's done, he may come back and try to snag another one. Because he says "thank you" as he's unwrapping his second lolly you don't try to stop him, but you're not so happy and wish the dad would say something.

   Now, when he grows up, hopefully he won't just continue to insincerely say what he thinks he has to say or do what he thinks he has to do as a means to get what he wants. Imagine *davening* everyday not to praise or thank Hashem for all He does, but simply to have Him throw a lolly (or shiny, new Acura) our way? How would He feel about that?

3. **The Genuine Article:** This is the child who knows that the Candy Man is not a paid position, and appreciates the treat. He comes, smiles and asks if he may have, then chooses quickly and says an audible and sincere thank you.

   These kids are a Candy Man's dream. This is the good boy or girl we want to reward with the lollipops, and it makes us remember why we do what we do. His sweetness is more tantalizing than the pop. As an adult, this is the type of person people will enjoy dealing with.

4. **The Sneak:** Usually found in older kids, this personality type manifests itself in a nonchalant sidling up to the Candy Man's side. There's a glance in every direction but that of the lollipop bag, then a snake-like hand quickly and stealthily makes its way into the bag and, with a single, lightning-quick motion, slides the captured sucker into his pocket as he steps away towards the back door. He thinks he is being sly and that the Candy Man didn't see. I saw, and it's pathetic. Again, all he had to do was ask and I'm happy to give him. Who does he think he's fooling?

   Now, as a grownup: what kind of human being will he be if he thinks he's getting away with things on his own, not acknowledging others who help him? What kind of shul concept will he have when he grows up? That it's a place to find goodies on your own? That's not how God works the last time I checked. Then, there is...

5. **The Eternal Optimist:** At first, I found this kid to be pesky, but then I realized how amazing his lolly-related trait is. This is the child who will come back time after time and ask for a lolly. "Didn't you already have one? (or two or three?!)"

Innocently, he nods his head in the affirmative. "Sorry, one per person," I say. And he walks away. A little later, he may be back. Or he'll do it again the next time he's at shul. Didn't he get the point? Why does he keep asking?

Then I noticed something. When I said, "No" he was fine with it. He didn't pout, didn't try to "hondle" or negotiate with me, he just smiled and walked away. Wow!

Here was a kid who understood that the Candy Man could make him happy, understood when the answer was no, and never got discouraged. He always thought that maybe, just maybe, this was the time he'd get four lollies when he asked.

You know what? I wanted to keep that spirit alive so the next time he asked for an extra lolly — after the licorice and the first lolly — I said, "Yes!" and gave it to him.

For a grown-up, this is probably the ultimate attitude to have for a happy life and meaningful shul experience. When he gets good things, he will be full of joy and appreciation. When he doesn't, he'll be just as okay and won't get depressed when he hears, "No," whether from his boss, his spouse, friends, or *HaKadosh Baruch Hu*. He knows that everything he gets is a treat that he doesn't deserve, and will revel in the joy of getting things and not get bogged down with depression when he misses out.

As a *davener*, he will constantly ask Hashem for things and not give up no matter how many times Hashem says "No," because he knows that each day, maybe, just maybe, this will be the day he hears, "Yes!"

What Can I Do?

Job Guidance for a Career in Life

TIMES ARE TOUGH. ECONOMICALLY, we're experiencing one of the biggest bubble-bursts in decades, when unemployment is higher than it has been in half a century. I speak to many people and often they make a big mistake when they are looking for work.

"What do you want to do?" I ask.

"I'll do anything," or "I don't care as long as they pay me," they reply.

"I know," I persist, "but what do you like doing?"

"It doesn't matter," they insist. "I just need *parnasah*."

They are missing the point. *Parnasah* comes from Hashem. How you get it is up to you.

First of all, as an employer, if someone tells me he'll do anything, that's nebulous. I don't need you, there's a world of people out there who can do "anything." Tell me why YOU are special; why YOU are going to bring something to my business; why I need YOU. Be specific; be exact. Tell me why what you do is unique.

When I was first looking into the working world, wondering what I would do, my brother gave me a book called "What Color Is My Parachute?" It is a best seller and is revised every year. It helps you match your natural abilities and interests with current job opportunities and occupations. I recommend it if you need that sort of guidance.

In my case, I didn't follow through with the book. Instead, I took some courses in a computer field that was "the next hottest career market, where you'll make six figures within two years!" They were right about the six figures; they just didn't mention that one or two of them came *after* the decimal point.

So what happened? I didn't last. It wasn't something I loved and I was only doing it for the money. Because of that, I wasn't happy in what I was doing and the money never materialized either. Had I initially thought about what I enjoyed or what I was good at, I might have made a different career choice, as I did less than a year later. Years later, I found out that this wasn't only the good advice of the author of that book, but I learned that this was the guidance of the Chovos HaLevavos.

He writes that each person is imbued with unique inclinations, interests, and skills, and he should use these as the source for his livelihood. One should not say, "I'll go into that profession because they make a lot of money," because *parnasah* comes from the *Ribono shel Olam* and He can make a person wealthy or poor in any field. Think about it, how many people became wealthy on junk, leftovers, and closeouts, and how many starving lawyers and Wall Street financiers are there?

So, if you are in need of a job, follow the advice of Rabbeinu Bachya ibn Paquda and seek out something that matches your natural inclinations, as Hashem has instilled them in you, and have faith that He can sustain you in whatever field you choose. Remembering that no one else can help you or harm you unless Hashem decrees it, will also make you more accepting of each situation and help you cope with the challenges. (*Davening* helps too!)

Now, I'm not just writing this to help people who are out of work. No, this has broader implications as well. You see, in any situation in life, we will find that certain abilities of ours will rise to the forefront or shine in a moment of darkness. What we need to do is find those natural strengths with which *HaKadosh Baruch Hu* blessed us and use them to serve Him.

I remember a conversation I had with a friend in yeshivah, Eliyahu K. I had decided that I had to buckle down and stop being such a joker. I was going to become solemn and serious. Eliyahu noticed this and said to me, "Hashem makes people different. Some people are meant to be serious, some are meant to be jokers. You have to live up to whom He wanted you to be. Jonny, Hashem didn't intend for you to be serious!"

I knew he was right and I stopped trying to be something I wasn't. Now, I wouldn't call myself a *leitz*, who makes fun of and ridicules everything, but I definitely try to see the funny and lighter side of things. Making people smile and be *b'simchah* is part of my genetic and spiritual makeup, and I think people appreciate it.

Some people are gifted with their hands, some are able to assess others' moods and speak soothingly to them. Some people are analytical; some are artistic. All these various abilities are given to us to seek out and determine the color of *our* parachutes, those lifelines which were put into our *neshamos* by the Creator. Once we figure that out, we have to pull the ripcord and put them to use.

There's one more aspect to being specific that I wanted to bring out. I believe R' Paysach Krohn was the mind behind this next thought. It's an insightful approach to helping others. Often, when others are in need, be it physical, financial, or emotional, we want to help. We tell them, "If there's anything I can do, just call." Says Rabbi Krohn, "That's worthless! They're not going to call you and ask you to do something because they don't know what you will be willing to do. They don't know your capabilities or your inclination to help."

"Instead," says R' Paysach, "be specific. Say, 'I can drive you to the hospital to visit your loved one in the mornings,' that way, they'll call you when they need a ride. Or say, 'You know, I can't drive you to the hospital, but your kids can come to my house from school for an hour so you can get some rest.' These are things people can actually take you up on, not some vague offer that will never be acted upon."

Just like the employer who should be told what you can do for him, in life we need to identify the things we can do and act on them. Make the effort to find opportunities for *chesed*. Avraham Avinu didn't take in guests because they needed help; he sought them out because *he* needed to help!

Find your talents and see how you can use them to make the world a better place. Then do it. Your career in living offers the ultimate job security because as long as you're alive you've got things to accomplish.

The World's DUH-mest Headline

I AM NOT A FAN of the news. First of all, it's usually quite depress-ing and full of things you shouldn't hear about. Murders, bankruptcies, stabbings, riots, ginger ale and cake boxes strewn about — horrible things. It's not really important for most of us, and has little relevance to any of our lives. My feeling is that if God wants me to find out about it I will.

For example, politics. I don't stand around pontificating about who should be president, what Israel should do, what Congress should do for Israel (although I have sent e-mails to the president and vice-president asking them to pardon Jonathan Pollard). Why don't I do these things? Because so far, none of them has asked for my advice. Believe me, the day Barack Obama or Bibi Netanyahu call me, I'll get up to speed really quickly and ask Daas Torah for guidance.

Besides, since "*Lev melachim v'sarim b'yad Hashem* — the hearts of kings and princes (and of course, presidents) are in the hand of Hashem," they can't do anything other than what He tells them to do. If you're really concerned about the world and how it's run, forget the president, speak to his Boss.

Anyway, I am therefore not often caught up in the news nor do I scrutinize every headline. However, one happened to cross my path and I just had to write about it. As I said, if Hashem wants me to find out about it, I will.

The news item was the unfortunate tale of a disturbed young

man in Nebraska who opened fire at a shopping mall, killing a number of people and then himself. But tragic as it was, that's not what caught my eye. What piqued my interest was the headline I saw:

"Shooter in Nebraska Mall Massacre Felt Worthless."

I have only one word — DUH! Come on, do you think you need to tell us that he felt worthless? I mean, when was the last time someone with healthy self-esteem said, "Boy, I'm feeling really great about myself today. Let me do something horrible that will have tragic impact and severe repercussions on dozens of lives"? Never, because when people feel good about themselves, they want to keep doing good and being good.

Now, some of you may point to people willing to blow themselves up to hurt others, but under normal circumstances, that isn't the case, and you don't find the people who tell their followers how wonderful it is to be martyred taking their own advice. They somehow live to see another day.

The *yetzer hara* has many tools in his arsenal, but one of the most powerful is the feeling of worthlessness. Think about it, when a person gets depressed, he starts thinking that he doesn't matter. If he doesn't matter, then neither does anyone else. Nor do his actions matter.

It becomes a vicious downward spiral where he can continue to fall further and further and almost nothing can stop him. Why should he stop? What's the point?

We all run into this feeling on occasion. "My boss will disparage my work anyway, why bother trying for perfection?" "My husband/wife will criticize my clothes and my looks anyway so why should I take care of myself?" "I'll never do well in school so why bother trying?" They may not be true, but we let those thoughts control us.

How many of us have heard someone say, "I'm worth more dead than alive," or "At least if I died my family would have the insurance money"? These expressions of worthlessness are the edge of a slippery slope from which there may be no return, like there wasn't for the young man from Nebraska. What can we do?

Fight these feelings right away.

If we see the ploy for what it is, a trick to get us to sink lower, then it's easier to haul ourselves back up again. If we recognize that when we're depressed the mood will likely change tomorrow, and we make sure not to act on it, we're already part-way to the cure.

So, when I read that the gunman felt worthless? Tell me something I don't know. Tell me about the man who felt worthless, and instead of shooting up a store, school, or post office, he decided to make something of himself.

Tell me about Shmuel Greenbaum whose wife of sixteen months was killed in the Sbarro bombing in 2001. Instead of wallowing in his depression and doing nothing, he decided to take an active role in making the world a better place and began a newsletter which highlights acts of kindness and promotes the furtherance of *chesed* to people around the world. Today, he has thousands of readers of his daily e-mails and a forthcoming book. THAT'S something to report.

But it doesn't have to be that grandiose. It can be a small achievement that maybe nobody else in the world knows about. I'd like to see the story of the man who came home in a really bad mood after being fired but covered it up and acted normal so his wife wouldn't know what was happening until he had a plan. Or maybe the story of the woman who was feeling washed out and tired of life who nevertheless made sure her children saw her with a smile on her face. I would find that personal strength noteworthy.

We can take it down a notch, too. If one were to find themselves depressed and feeling down and told themselves it would pass so they rolled over and went to sleep, that would be a tremendous thing! They'd be telling the *yetzer hara* that they're wise to his tricks and won't be party to what he has in mind.

And if someone who never thought they could do any of these things is inspired by this article and overcomes his or her own negative feelings? THAT should make headlines.

In the Blink of an Eye

*T*HERE'S A FAMOUS EXPRESSION: *"Yeshuas Hashem k'heref ayin —* Hashem's salvation is like the blink of an eye." I'm not really sure of its source, but it is well accepted and oft-quoted.

Usually, people use it when someone is in pain, suffering tremendous pressure, or going through some great difficulty. Hashem's salvation comes quickly, they say, in the blink of an eye. What a person is going through today could be entirely reversed tomorrow. That thought is comforting, but many of us are skeptical.

Things didn't get this way overnight, how can they get better overnight? The answer is that we don't have to know how they can getter, just that they can. When the King of Aram besieged Shomron, Elisha told the King of Yisrael that the famine was about to end and that the next day food would be very inexpensive. The King's general was skeptical and said it was impossible. Elisha said, "You will live to see it, but you will not eat from it."

As we all know, the four *metzora'im* walked into the camp of Aram that night and found it was empty. Hashem had sent an angel to scare off the besieging soldiers and the entire camp and all its contents were left behind. As the *Navi* had predicted, food was very cheap and available by the next day. The general witnessed it but was trampled to death shortly thereafter by the hungry people rushing to get food.

He could not imagine a way for Hashem to intercede so he

doubted it could be done. It happened in a way he could not imagine. Want more? How about another case?

Hashem told Moshe that *Klal Yisrael* would eat meat for thirty days. Moshe wondered how Hashem would achieve such a feat. Hashem got angry at him, asking, "Is God's hand short [of ability]?" A totally unexpected occurrence took place and wave upon wave of birds flew in. The Jews did indeed have enough meat for a month.

How about a modern-day version? A fellow needed money to make a wedding. He went to the bank to get a loan, but knew he had no collateral and doubted he would be successful. As he walked into his local branch, he met a well-to-do Jew who was known to be a pillar of his community. "Do you have an account here?" asked the *gevir*. When he said that he did, he was told that the bank was going public and accountholders got first chance to buy shares.

"I don't have money to buy any shares," lamented the poor father of the bride. "That's okay," said the wealthy man. "I will give you money for shares, and I will then buy them from you at a profit." The money he was paid for his shares paid for the wedding.

"If you told me Hashem was 100% going to send me the money," he later recounted, "and asked me how He was going to do it, I would never have thought of this in a million years."

What seems interesting is that Hashem's salvation is not only quick, but unpredictable. I was thinking about the comparison to the "blink of an eye." What happens when you blink?

Well, if we think about it in slow motion it will be easier. First, your eyelid begins to close. Things get progressively darker until you can't see anything. You're blind. Now what happens? Nourishment!

Your eye gets the moisture it needs to maintain its vision. That infusion of fluids also gives your eye a momentary respite from the constant toil of focusing and unfocusing. It relaxes the eye somewhat, and rejuvenates it.

The next moment, your eyelid pops open and everything is brilliantly bright again. In fact, you see better than you did before.

The more I think about it, the more I understand the comparison of Hashem's salvation to the blink of an eye. If I wanted to see better, my instinct would be to open my eye wider to let in more light. Instead, Hashem made us so that the eye begins to shut. We then might think, "Okay, I'll squint," but the eye closes all the way. Only after that does it open to let in light and we can see better than before, thanks to the momentary lapse in sight.

The same is true in our lives. We often find ourselves trying to improve our situation, whether financially, in our relationships, our health, or anything else you can imagine. Sometimes it seems that the harder we try to open the door wide, the narrower and smaller it gets until finally it seems to slam in our faces.

If we get upset and curse our bad luck, we would do well to remember "*Yeshuas Hashem k'heref ayin* — Hashem's salvation is like the blink of an eye." What we think is darkening and detrimental often turns out to be the prelude to our getting the nourishment and improved situation we were hoping for.

And I think that's the point. We don't tell someone who is having a hard time that Hashem's salvation is like the blink of an eye simply to say that it can be over very quickly. That's helpful also, but the message is much deeper and uplifting.

Just like the blink of an eye which results in bright, wide-open eyes, Hashem's salvation begins with a constriction. That means that Hashem isn't just responsible for the rescue, but for the difficulty too — and it's all part of one big Master plan!

When you are suffering financial straits, emotional hardships, or spiritual struggles, the point is to nourish you and help you to be stronger; to give you clearer vision and a brighter future. That's the encouragement we offer someone in times of trouble.

Yes, things are difficult, and yes you can't see a way out. But, remember that we wouldn't think that closing our eyes would help us see better either. In fact, when we restrict our own vision, and trust that Hashem is behind all that befalls us and everything we are fortunate enough to receive, that's when we are really seeing with clarity.

Get a Job

A S A WRITER, I am often asked to help people with resumes. Often, they have no idea how to go about it, and give me a list of everything they've done before, including primary education and babysitting positions. I ask them what they're looking for and they say, "a job." If they have given it some thought, they respond, "a good job."

I try to explain that in order to write a resume they need to have an idea of what they want to do. "It doesn't matter; I can do lots of different jobs." I once helped a young woman who listed customer service work in her past employment history. Knowing her to be the type of person who doesn't like dealing with people's problems, I asked if she was looking for a customer-service position. She responded that she wasn't but that she thought it showed her to be more well-rounded; that it "sounded good." I pulled it out. Don't offer something you're not willing to do. Just ignore it.

Last year, I was asked to help someone make a resume for his first job post-*kollel*. He gave me his yeshivah history, as well as some summer work experience. I asked what kind of job he wanted. He didn't know and didn't care. He had a few preferences but nothing major. He wanted freedom, and not much structure. Okay, that was obvious. I asked about his skills, and bowling came up. It was going nowhere fast.

Let me give you some advice: If you are looking for a job, don't focus on the job, but on yourself. If you are averse to heavy-lifting, don't wear a bulky jacket trying to look strong enough to get a job delivering appliances. If you hate numbers, don't go for an accounting degree just because "that's where they're hiring." What's the point of getting a job doing something you don't like?

Now, you may say you're trying to fulfill the curse of Adam HaRishon to work hard, but you don't really have to do that. *Chazal* direct us to find jobs that are easy and clean, that are prestigious and honest. There are plenty of other references to the kind of job a person should choose, too. Everyone has his or her own natural abilities and we should look to utilize them.

No less a personage than the Chovos HaLevavos said that a person should seek a job which makes him happy and suits his talents. Wanna make the big bucks? Here's how: Look around and determine which jobs are paying the most money. Now put that list away, and see what jobs would be a good fit for your nature. Hashem doesn't need you to be a hotshot financier or oil baron to make money. He has plenty of ways to do it, so don't make yourself crazy.

Instead, focus on what you're good at, and what good you can do, and follow that. The best resume follows this principle: Don't focus on what you've done, but on what you want to do in the future.

Now, why write about this topic? I'm not running a recruiting business or a placement service. I'm trying to bring out an important point. The fellow who didn't know what he was looking for couldn't find a job until he set some goals. The girl who included what she thought others wanted to hear would have ended up with offers that didn't match what she was looking for.

In order to make progress in anything, we need solid goals and a good work ethic. We need to understand ourselves and our talents and use them to figure out our mission in life. The idea is not just to be busy, but to be useful.

In essence, Life itself is a job. Whether we're involved in our *parnasah*, our learning, our families, our interaction with others, or anything else, it has to be a "real" job, serving Hashem. Our Boss is very generous, but at the end of the day He wants to see results. We must figure out what we want to do and then do it. We can't let little things stop us such as laziness, confusion, or other people's opinions.

The secret of success is to picture your ultimate outcome, then live your life that way. Don't settle just because you can. I remember something my father said to me when I was eighteen or nineteen. I had made an arrangement with a Travel Agency to sell plane tickets in yeshivah and made a whopping ten dollars a ticket. I told him I might want to work there in the summer and then look into being an agent full-time.

He got annoyed with me and said, "What am I supposed to do, tell everyone about 'my son the travel agent?!'" Now, if you enjoy travel and helping people, you have a knack for organizing trips and tours, and you're okay with the schedule, then being a travel agent is a great *parnasah* for you. But I knew he meant something else.

I thought I'd be a travel agent because it sounded like an easy way to make money (it's not). I wasn't concerned with the bigger picture of who I would become in my lifelong job as a Jew. That's what got him upset. He knew I was talking about ignoring my potential and taking it easy.

Today, he doesn't talk about his son "the travel agent." In fact, for the most part, I don't think he talks about my day job at all. What he talks about is how proud he is that I try inspiring others through my writing and speaking, attempting to use my God-given talents for the betterment of myself and mankind. I'm so grateful for that one quick remark he made so many years ago.

I don't know if I'm successful in inspiring others, but I do know that I am trying (very trying, some of you might say). I'm constantly striving to inspire myself, too, and become a better person. Trust me, I've got my work cut out for me.

I'm hopeful that this article has given you some insights as well, some direction and guidance for the job of living. Don't focus on what you've done, but on what you want to do in the future.

Here's a quick test to determine whether you've completed everything you're supposed to in this life: If you're alive — you haven't.

More Lessons from the Candy Man

A S YOU MAY REMEMBER from earlier articles, I am the Candy Man in my shul. I buy treats for the children with my own money as do most Candy Men I know. (Remember this parents: These are not "gimmes" from the shul, kids need to say thank you and stick to whatever rules are put in place.) That means I get to choose what to give out.

Recently, I bought an assortment of candies and put them in a large jar at my seat. I had taffies, lollipops and winkies/fizzers/rockets/whateverelseyoucallthosesugarbuttons. I thought that most kids would stop and marvel at the choices and agonize over the decision. But I was wrong.

Time after time, the kids came over, looked into the jar, then reached in and grabbed a specific thing. I thought the taffies would be least favorite as they were the smallest and would be eaten the fastest, but I was wrong. It seemed the kids knew what they wanted and didn't give thought to whether something else would last longer. I learned some things that I'd like to share with everyone:

1. Different strokes for different folks.

Everyone has their own opinions about what tastes best, and they know themselves. I thought one treat would be more popular and I was wrong. Projection means we assume other people think like we do, and are bothered by the same things or have the same difficulties. They don't. We can't assume to know or understand someone else's motives because we are all different.

That's an important lesson for life. Just because I think one way, doesn't mean I can force my way of thinking onto someone else, or condemn someone who disagrees. Just because I'd have difficulty making up my mind doesn't mean someone else will, and that's fine. We're all different, and that's what keeps the world moving. By recognizing that others are capable where we fall short means we can find the value in everyone.

I remember when I had to fix my fence. I had no clue where to begin. As I often say, "My strengths lie elsewhere." If you need a speech for a *sheva brachos* in Bangladesh I can probably help you, but if you ask me about repairing something my eyes start to glaze over.

I asked a neighbor for advice about whom I should call for help. When he asked me if I had a sawhorse, I knew he was being optimistic and I'm pretty sure that by my blank stare he could tell this wasn't going to be easy. In a few minutes, he had unloaded a bunch of tools from his garage and the job was done. As they say, good neighbors make good fences.

I could never have done what he did but that doesn't mean I begrudge him or feel inferior. *Baruch Hashem*, he can do what I can't, and maybe I can do some things he can't. That's as it should be.

When we see people who don't think the same way we do, or focus on the same mitzvos we do, we must also be forgiving. Some people can't seem to get to shul on time, while others can't stand being thirty seconds late. Some people think the most important mitzvah out there is being friendly to everyone even if it means saying or doing certain things a Jew ought not to. Others think you are nobody if you don't go to a *shiur*, and the list goes on. We all have different priorities; we need to understand and accept people for who they are. And we should savor the differences and nuances — candy wouldn't be as much fun if it was all the same flavor.

2. Focus on being happy, not happier.

I realized that my problem with the decision regarding the candies would be that I would think: "Well, I like this candy better, but this one will last longer, and that one can be eaten part now and part later..." and so on.

In essence, I wasn't choosing a candy, but the sensation I would get from the candy. I would weigh the various factors and suddenly give the control of my happiness into the "hands" of a sugar confection. The kids would see something that they would be happy with and take it. Case closed, end of story. They wanted something sweet, got it, and were happy.

They don't know enough yet to weigh the decision and think that while this would make them happy, maybe something else would make them happier. In this case, I'd have to agree that ignorance is bliss. Advertising constantly tells us that this will make us happy, that will make us loved, and the other thing will give us the satisfaction we've always wanted and needed.

The truth is, that's all baloney. Nothing can make you happy; happiness comes from your decision to see the good in what you have. Constantly looking outside ourselves causes untold problems. People look with envy at other people's possessions or lifestyles and wish they had it, or something just like it. Not only can't they have what other people do, they can no longer be happy with what they had and often end up losing everything.

We need to learn the lesson of these guileless children who take a candy and are happy with it, not concerned that maybe they should have picked another one. Savoring the sweetness of what we have instead of chewing on the bitterness of what we don't can make even us grown-ups happy, too.

In fact, the two lessons merge when we recognize that though we're different, we can bond by looking for the goodness in each other instead of the noting the shortcomings. When we enjoy the taffy's flavorful sticky chew and don't think about the fact that it will be done sooner, we are happy. Looking longingly at the stick of a lollipop and wishing our taffy had one won't make it so; it will only reduce the pleasure of the taffy.

So take a lesson from the Candy Man and look for the goodness in what you have and in the people around you. Then you'll see... how sweet it is.

ABOUT SURVIVAL THROUGH EDUCATION

Survival Through Education Inc., a 501(c)3 not-for-profit organization, aims to provide all Jews, regardless of affiliation, with a meaningful sense of Jewish pride and identity.

Our goal is to ensure Jewish survival through multiple streams of education, which speak to Jewish Heritage, History and Culture, utilizing text based learning, as well as hands-on application.

Over the years, Survival Through Education has distributed thousands of "*Seforim* of Substance" to the wider Jewish world and has been gratified to receive reports of increased Jewish pride from the recipients.

This has led to a deeper connection to Judaism and further manifested itself through increased involvement in Jewish life. Be it a commitment to refraining from eating *chametz* on Passover, to marrying within the faith, to a return to a fully Torah-observant lifestyle, Survival Through Education believes it is not our job to change the individual but rather to "Help the Chosen People Choose"©

The book you are holding in your hand is a partial result of the efforts of Survival through Educations Inc.'s efforts to bring quality Torah literature to Jews of all affiliations. If you are a writer, publisher, reader or supporter of quality Jewish literature and would like information on how we can help each other make *the* difference, please reach out to us at www.survivalthrougheducation.org or 718-983-9272.